Oppenheimer and the Atomic Bomb

OPPENHEIMER

and the Atomic Bomb

by Rebecca Larsen

Franklin Watts
New York London Toronto Sydney
1988

Library of Congress Cataloging in Publication Data

Larsen, Rebecca.
Oppenheimer and the atomic bomb / by Rebecca Larsen.
p. cm.
Bibliography: p.
Includes index.
Summary: Traces the life of the physicist who headed the Manhattan
Project which developed the first atomic bomb.
ISBN 0-531-10607-1
1. Oppenheimer, J. Robert, 1904–1967—Juvenile literature.
2. Atomic bomb—United States—History—Juvenile literature.
3. Manhattan Project (U.S.)—History—Juvenile literature.
4. Physicists—United States—Biography—Juvenile literature.
[1. Oppenheimer, J. Robert, 1904–1967. 2. Physicists. 3. Manhattan
Project (U.S.) 4. Atomic bomb.] I.Title.
QC16.O62L37 1988
623.4'5119'0924—dc19
[92]   88-16981 CIP AC

To my husband, Alan

Photographs courtesy of:
AP/Wide World Photos: pp. 2, 98, 102, 106, 107, 108, 109;
UPI/Bettmann Newsphotos: pp. 99, 100, 101, 103, 104, 105.

Contents

Oppenheimer and the Atomic Bomb

Introduction

A ball of fire a mile in diameter shot out of the desert horizon and changed colors as it boiled upward—first green, then deep purple, then orange, then green again. It was like viewing the corona of the sun during a total eclipse from a grandstand seat a few miles away.

Among the clusters of observers scattered at a safe distance from this fiery monster, the first atomic bomb, was J. Robert Oppenheimer. He was a tall, thin figure with unruly dark hair and intense blue eyes who had led a group of brilliant scientists in producing this terrible bomb that would end World War II.

At each step of his life, Oppenheimer faced challenges that read like the stuff of novels and movies. As a shy, tormented child genius, he struggled with his social clumsiness and physical weakness. As a college student and young instructor, he fought bouts of depression and struggled to find his role in the scientific world. On the atomic bomb project he faced political battles and the overwhelming scientific complexity of the task itself. After World War II he underwent political attacks over his alleged Communist Party affiliations and his waning faith in the government because of its drive to produce deadlier nuclear weapons.

At times Oppenheimer showed himself unequal to the struggle. He could be arrogant and bitingly sarcastic; there were many who felt he told lies and deceived friends. Although he was among the most brilliant of the nation's scientists, he devoted much of his energy to the Manhattan Project, which meant that he never made any discovery worthy of that coveted honor, the Nobel Prize.

But through his life runs a thread of strength and power. He took scanty materials, rudimentary knowledge, and a diverse, often egotistical group of scientists and molded the atomic bomb that opened a new age in science and technology. The morality and ethics of that task can be debated, but the fact remains that Oppenheimer and the bomb changed the face of life on this planet forever.

After the war Oppenheimer fought for peaceful uses of the bomb and for scientists to have a say over how their discoveries were used. He might not have achieved his goals, but he opened a pathway of involvement in politics and government that scientists still follow.

1

"An abnormally, repulsively good little boy"

J. Robert Oppenheimer sat at the front window of his parents' New York City apartment and peered down at the trains puffing along tracks below, the ferryboats sailing back and forth on the Hudson River.

The gritty big-city life of the early 1900s seemed worlds removed from the one he lived eleven floors above Riverside Drive, a world that prized good manners and gracious living as well as the arts and intellectual pursuits.

The Oppenheimers did not spend their money flamboyantly, but the high-ceilinged rooms of their nine-room apartment were filled with fine European furniture and hung with original paintings by French Impressionists, Vuillard, van Gogh, and Derain. There was also money for a pet dachshund, a butler and maid, a summer house on Long Island, private schooling for Robert and his brother Frank, and occasional trips to Europe.

Visitors found the atmosphere of the Oppenheimer home subdued and correct, like an elegant restaurant. No wonder that Robert later called himself "an abnormal, repulsively good little boy" whose home allowed "no normally healthy way to be a bastard."[1]

Robert Oppenheimer's parents were both Jews with close ties to Europe. His father, Julius, had emigrated from Germany in 1888, at the age of seventeen, to join a cloth-importing company founded in New York by some of his relatives, who had earlier come to the United States. Young Julius arrived speaking scarcely any English and began his work in a lowly storeroom, where he unpacked and classified bolts of cloth. But he quickly rose to the top of the firm, which marketed fabric to line the insides of men's suits. As Julius grew more prosperous, he dressed like a banker, spoke excellent English, and developed a taste for the artistic.

His interest in art may well have been the reason that he proposed marriage to Ella Friedman, a young woman from a Bavarian family that had lived in the Philadelphia–Baltimore region for generations. At the time of her marriage to Julius she was a painter, teaching art in her own studio in New York. She was refined and delicate, not inclined to laugh or joke, and she made an accomplished and lovely bride for Julius.

There was an air of mystery and sorrow about Ella as well. Visitors to the Oppenheimer home always noticed the strange chamois glove that covered her right hand at all times. Although family members avoided discussing it, Ella had been born without a right hand. The glove disguised a primitive artificial hand.

About a year after the Oppenheimers' marriage, on a cold spring night, while a pneumonia epidemic gripped New York, Ella Friedman Oppenheimer gave birth to her first child, a son. The date was April 22, 1904.

After a long and difficult labor, the baby was born at his parents' home, which was then a gabled house on West 94th Street. Julius Oppenheimer at first decided to call the child Robert but then added his own initial at the front of his son's name—J. Robert. Whether or not it stood for Julius is debatable. Robert himself claimed it stood "for nothing."[2]

Several years later the family moved to the Riverside Drive apartment, where Robert's brother Frank was born in 1912. Even before entering school, Robert seemed interested in science. At the age of five he was taken to Germany, where his grandfather, Ben, gave him a small box holding some two dozen rock samples, all labeled in German. The gift turned Robert into an ardent mineral collector. By the age of eleven, when most boys are stumbling through schoolwork and spending their free time playing ball, he was elected to the prestigious New York Mineralogical Club, where he even gave lectures on his finds.

"When I was ten or twelve years old, minerals, writing poems and reading, and building with blocks still—architecture—were the three themes that I did," Oppenheimer said.[3]

From hunting and cataloging rocks Robert moved on to study crystallization and the refraction of light, using a microscope and a polarizer, a device that would create electromagnetic fields.

Although they were both Jews, Robert's parents did not belong to a temple. Instead they joined the Ethical Culture Society, founded by another German immigrant, Felix Adler, to promote nonsectarian or nonreligious ethical principles. Society members preached the need for stronger morality and believed that morality should not be based on religious dogma. They contended that humans could develop values that would allow them to live and die with dignity without the aid of religious institutions.

Adler had founded a school in New York City, on Central Park West, which Robert entered in second grade and attended through high school. From the very beginning he almost devoured his books and stood out even among the bright and wealthy children at the Ethical Culture School.

His Greek and Latin instructor, Alberta Newton, was surprised at his progress. "He received every new idea as perfectly beautiful," she said.[4] At age eleven Robert once challenged an older girl-cousin: "Ask me a question and I will answer you in Greek."[5]

His mathematics teacher, Matilda Auerbach, was upset with how restless Robert was in her class and sent him to the library to do advanced work on his own. Then Robert would return to explain to the other students what he'd learned.

One summer during his high school years Robert worked with the science teacher, Augustus Klock, to set up equipment for the following year's studies and to try out physics and chemistry experiments. Occasionally, the teacher and student would go off on mineral-collecting trips as a reward for Robert's work.

Because of Klock, Robert's love for chemistry grew. Years later he would tell people that if they wanted to get someone interested in science, "teach them elementary chemistry."[6]

Another teacher, Herbert Winslow Smith, who taught English at the Ethical Culture School, moved into Robert's life during the young man's high school years. Robert wrote an essay on oxygen for one of Smith's classes. "I think your vocation is to be a science writer," Smith said, after reading his pupil's work.[7] Robert didn't think so, but many years later he would recall Smith's words.

Even though Robert triumphed in his classes, like many intellectual students he bumbled through other areas of life. He had turned into a miniature professor who astounded adults and often antagonized other children. Tall, pencil-thin, and bushy-haired, he blushed easily and had difficulty making friends.

A classmate, Jane Kayser, remembers that as a teenager "he was still a little boy; he was very frail, very pink-cheeked, very shy, and very brilliant of course. Very quickly everybody admitted that he was different from all the others and very superior. As far as studies were concerned he was good in everything."[8]

Like many students who eat and drink books, Robert avoided sports and physical activity. He didn't even walk much; he was driven by car everywhere. Often he refused to use the stairs at school and instead rode the elevator. Finally, the angry school principal wrote a note home to his parents: "Please teach your son to walk upstairs; he is holding up class."[9]

After that the Oppenheimers tried to push Robert into sports, particularly after he suffered an attack of tubercular fever. Tennis was the rage, and Robert tried it. But he was gangly and uncoordinated like his father, and he quit because of his zeal for perfection. He hated doing anything that he couldn't do well, even on the tennis court.

One summer shortly after Robert turned fourteen, he went to a camp run mainly for boys from well-to-do families in New York City. Robert's dislike of physical sports, the way he showed off what he knew, and his refusal to fight back made the other boys call him names and torment him physically. On top of it all, Robert wrote a letter home to his parents telling them that he was glad he had come to camp because he was finally learning the facts of life. His shocked parents rushed to the camp for a visit with the administrators, and soon afterward camp officials cracked down on boys for sharing dirty stories. The other campers were furious at Robert and locked him naked in an icehouse overnight.

All of this didn't mean, however, that Robert lacked physical courage or feared danger. At Bay Shore on Long Island, where the Oppenheimers had their summer home, Robert and his brother, Frank, sailed eagerly on a twenty-eight-foot sloop named the *Trimethy*. Not surprisingly, the precocious boys had named the vessel after a chemical compound, trimethylamine (CHN), a colorless liquid that smelled like pickled herring. Together the brothers plied the rough waves while their mother hovered anxiously, watching them from the window of their summer house.

Robert and a school friend, Paul Horgan, often went out on the sloop to anchor in the shallow part of Great South Bay.

A typical afternoon might find Horgan working at his type-writer, tapping out bad imitations of the Russian playwright Chekhov and other short story writers, while in the cockpit Robert sat avidly savoring a book on thermodynamics.

One day the two sailed too close to the Fire Island inlet as the tide was going out, and in just three minutes the current caught the boat and began to sweep it toward the ocean. A great storm had just ended, and enormous breakers still crashed at the mouth of the inlet. For two hours Robert struggled to bring the boat back. He tacked back and forth, back and forth, until finally the *Trimethy* seemed to reach safety.

Meanwhile, on shore, the Oppenheimer family waited in panic, and Mr. Oppenheimer coerced a local revenue cutter into beginning a search. As the *Trimethy* bobbed back across the bay at about eleven at night, Paul and Robert spotted the big boat hunting for them. They were taken aboard and fed and warmed up, a happy ending to an adventure that could have ended in disaster.

In February 1921 Robert graduated from Ethical Culture with straight As and prepared to enter Harvard in the autumn with a school friend, Francis Fergusson, who came from Albuquerque, New Mexico.

As a postgraduation celebration Robert and his family traveled to Germany, where he went off into the Harz Mountains to hunt minerals. He returned with a suitcase full of rocks and a bad case of dysentery, which turned into colitis, a digestive problem that would plague him for the rest of his life. Harvard and all of Robert's grand plans were postponed. He spent the winter recuperating at his parents' apartment, where he grew depressed and rebellious and ever more angry at his anxious parents.

In the spring Julius Oppenheimer begged Herbert Winslow Smith, the popular English teacher from Ethical Culture, to take Robert out West on a trip to revive his health and spirits. Smith, who had traveled to New Mexico with another student the summer before, took Robert to Cowles, a small community twenty miles up the Pecos Valley in the Sangre de Cristo Mountains northeast of Santa Fe.

There the two stayed at Los Pinos, a remote, yet elite guest ranch run by Katherine Chaves Page and her husband, Winthrop. Robert developed a crush on Katherine Page and also fell in love with New Mexico, a love that would last his whole life. In spite of his frailty Robert became an expert horseman. He surprised the New Mexicans with his endurance as he and Smith roamed the mountains of Colorado and New Mexico. Over the campfires Robert's friendship with Smith grew to be a deep bond. For years to come, as he climbed through educational institutions and traveled the world, Robert would write letters to his beloved teacher.

The trip changed Robert's life and eventually would have a lasting impact on national and world events. It introduced Robert to the mountains and valleys of New Mexico, an area that would play a major role in his future scientific work and the fate of the nation. The pine trees, broad horizons, and uninhabited wilderness deeply impressed Robert. New Mexico opened up his world and also invigorated him, preparing him for the years of study to come. He returned to the East Coast refreshed and ready to begin his studies at Harvard.

2

"Much kinder and more tolerant"

When Robert Oppenheimer arrived at a freshman dormitory on the Charles River at Harvard University in the fall of 1922, like most college freshmen he didn't have a completely clear idea about what field he would major in, although he leaned toward chemistry. When he asked a friend at Harvard whether he should study chemistry or mineralogy (with the idea of becoming a mining engineer because he loved his trips into mountains and caves hunting for rocks), the friend told him, "Study chemistry; there are always summer vacations."[1]

Although chemistry attracted him, he threw himself into other areas that showed he could as easily have been a writer as a scientist. He studied French prose and poetry and the history of philosophy; he joined the Student Liberal Club, which attracted those upset with how World War I had been resolved in Europe; he wrote poems and short stories. One of his stories was about a young mining engineer who at first thinks he's too sophisticated for the "miserable miners" but later becomes afraid that he will one day end up like the superintendent of the mine, a man who is a college graduate just like him.[2]

Oppenheimer sent much of this fiction to his former teacher, Herbert Smith, to be critiqued. There is no record that any of it was ever published.

Oppenheimer probably never dated a girl while he was at all-male Harvard, although girls from Vassar, Wellesley, and Radcliffe were often on the campus. One friend said Oppenheimer and his circle of friends were all too much in love with intellectual life, philosophy, science, and the arts to be thinking about girls. One friend, Jeffries Wyman, said, "We were good friends, and he had some other friends, but there was something that he lacked, perhaps some more personal and deep emotional contact with people than we were having, because our contacts were largely, I should say wholly, on an intellectual basis."[3]

Not just his intellectual life held Oppenheimer back from being more social. He was beginning to have bouts of depression, which would trouble him throughout his school years.

The first hint that Oppenheimer might be leaning away from chemistry and toward physics came in his freshman year, when he applied to take graduate-level physics courses without having taken undergraduate courses first. To back up his application he submitted an impressive list of physics books he had read on his own, including *Thermodynamics and Statistical Mechanics, On the Equilibria of Heterogeneous Systems,* and *Atombau u. Spectral-linien.*

His petition was granted, although one professor joked, "Obviously if he says he's read these books he's a liar, but he should get a Ph.D. for knowing these titles."[4]

As Oppenheimer passed through Harvard, he took six courses at a time so that he could graduate in three years. In most he earned As, but there were occasional Bs. One of Oppenheimer's friends claims that when one physics professor realized that he had given an A in a tough elementary thermodynamics course to a student carrying six courses, he decided his class was too easy and made it harder the next year.

At Harvard, Oppenheimer studied with Professor Percy W. Bridgman, an experimental physicist who began turning Oppenheimer's thoughts toward studying physics further after graduation. Under Bridgman he began a small experiment on the effect of pressure on the resistance of alloys.

But Oppenheimer, brilliant at mathematics and in thinking up problems, was almost as awkward and clumsy in manipulating materials in a laboratory as he was handling a racquet on the tennis court. He persevered, however, and picked up from Bridgman's lab assistant much of the information he needed to do the experiments, but he told friends that he wasn't sure he was cut out for experimental science.

In spite of that, after graduating from Harvard he applied to the University of Cambridge in England, where he hoped to work at the famed Cavendish Laboratory with Professor Sir Ernest Rutherford. Cambridge was one of three main centers of atomic research in Europe at the time. The others were the University of Copenhagen, Denmark, the kingdom of Niels Bohr, and the University of Göttingen in Germany, the headquarters for Max Born, James Franck, and David Hilbert.

Nobel Prize winner Rutherford, often called the father of nuclear science, evolved the nuclear theory that is widely accepted today. He suggested that the atom contains a tiny nucleus at its center, which is positively charged and holds all protons of the atom and therefore almost all of its mass. Very light, negatively charged electrons make up the outer regions.

But Rutherford was too advanced for Oppenheimer. Because the twenty-one-year-old Oppenheimer had limited courses in physics and lacked some major scientific project of his own to work on, he was assigned to work instead in the Cambridge laboratory of another famous physicist, Sir Joseph J. Thomson. Thomson had won the Nobel prize for proving the existence of the electron.

Presumably, Oppenheimer did need more experience in the laboratory. Even the simple task of soldering two copper wires together would frustrate him. The day-to-day grind in the laboratory wore him down as he realized how limited his experimental ability was. The very idea that he might fail ate away at him over the next few months.

At one point he wrote to his old friend from New Mexico, Francis Fergusson: "The lab work is a terrible bore, and I am so bad at it that it is impossible to feel that I am learning anything."[5]

Thomson set him to work in a large basement laboratory preparing very thin films of beryllium, a strong yet brittle metallic element used mainly as a hardening agent in alloys. The films were to be used by another physicist in investigating the penetrating power of electrons. Oppenheimer remembered later: "The business in the laboratory was really quite a sham but it got me into the laboratory where I heard talk and found out a good deal of what people were interested in. I still had the feeling that I should be able to understand what was going on in metals, but, of course, I didn't."[6]

By then several of Oppenheimer's friends from Harvard who had gone on to study in England were getting worried about him. Desperately lonely and convinced that his friends were deserting him, Oppenheimer read the deep and dark novels of Dostoevsky and Proust and fretted over his failures. At Christmas of that year Oppenheimer took a holiday in Brittany in France. He walked along the seashore and thought about suicide. "I was on the point of bumping myself off," he told others later.

He also had a rather bizarre holiday reunion in Paris with Francis Fergusson. During the course of an ordinary conversation Oppenheimer suddenly jumped on Fergusson and seemed ready to strangle him. Fergusson managed to fend off the attack; Oppenheimer immediately apologized and later tried to explain his strange behavior.

Back in Cambridge, Oppenheimer began seeing a psychiatrist. "It was obvious," said one of his friends, "there was a tremendous inner turmoil, in spite of which he kept on doing a tremendous amount of work, thinking, reading, discussing things, but obviously with a sense of great inner anxiety and alarm."[7]

At just the right moment, though, Oppenheimer traveled with friends to the island of Corsica, a holiday that proved to be a turning point in his terrible year in the laboratory. For ten days they hiked the full length of the island and slept in small inns and peasant huts or out in the open. The vacation proved just the right medicine for the troubled student. He returned to England refreshed and told his friends that he knew more about his troubles than his doctor did, and he would handle them himself.

In later life Oppenheimer told others that this black time of testing had improved and changed him. He felt that as a result he became "much kinder and more tolerant—able to form satisfactory, sensible relationships."

And although Oppenheimer was frustrated with laboratory work, he was finding a place for himself in theoretical physics. Among the people Oppenheimer met in England was Max Born, director of the Institute of Theoretical Physics at the University of Göttingen in Germany. Born invited him to continue his work in Göttingen. "I felt completely relieved of the responsibility to go back into a laboratory," Oppenheimer said. "I hadn't been good, I hadn't done anybody any good, and I hadn't had any fun whatever; and here was something I felt just driven to try."[8]

In spite of his clumsiness with wires and films and test tubes, Oppenheimer was becoming known for brilliance in physics and for his sharp wit. Even his physical appearance made him the center of attention: his lanky, slouching figure, penetrating blue eyes, and wild dark hair. He wore expensive, impeccably tailored clothing and had perfect table manners.

In a soft yet clear voice he talked around the dinner table as much about literature and the exotic writers of the West and East as he did about physics.

When Oppenheimer arrived at Göttingen in 1926, he found a sleepy, antiquated-looking town of half-timbered houses and carved beams. Beneath the outward dreaminess of the city the scientific world of the university teemed with new ideas that were revolutionizing the original quantum theory of physics. The old theory worked out by the German physicist Max Planck explained that atoms absorbed and emitted energy in small chunks or particles of electromagnetic radiation known as quanta.

The theory had been very useful to such scientists as Albert Einstein and Niels Bohr in explaining the structure of the atom, but it needed some elaboration to explain several atomic phenomena. In the 1920s physicists in several European centers began to extend the theory into a new one, known as quantum mechanics. In particular, quantum mechanics rested on the theories of German physicist Erwin Schrödinger, who proposed a new model of the atom.

In universities such as Göttingen there were constant conferences and debates, arguments and calculations, as scientists struggled to understand the structure of the atom. Although Oppenheimer was one of the youngest on the scene, he was accepted largely because of two of his papers on quantum theory that a Cambridge journal had published just before he arrived in Göttingen.

In Göttingen, Oppenheimer met many of the famous European scientists. He continued work he had begun in England on applications of the quantum theory, and wrote the dissertation for his Ph.D on the basis of this work. He also studied scattering, the changes in the path and velocity of two or more atomic particles when they collide.

Toward the end of his time at Göttingen, Oppenheimer had a run-in with the German bureaucracy, which was well known for stubbornly enforcing rules. When he applied to take an exam to get his Ph.D., the Prussian Ministry of Education turned him down. The university asked why and was told that "Herr Oppenheimer made a wholly inadequate application . . ." in applying to the university for acceptance. He had neglected to include a detailed account of his career and therefore had never formally been admitted.[9] His professors pleaded his case and in fact insisted that he could not afford to stay in Germany any longer, a fairly unlikely story. At any rate, the ministry gave in, and Oppenheimer successfully took his oral examination in May 1927.

His work on his dissertation finished, Oppenheimer, who had once faltered in the laboratory and seemed on the brink of failure, suddenly found himself wooed like a celebrity by American universities anxious to hire instructors who knew the latest in physics coming out of Europe.

Ultimately, he decided to take a job at the University of California at Berkeley, precisely because that school had only the beginnings of a physics department. "I visited Berkeley and thought I'd like to go to Berkeley because it was a desert. There was no theoretical physics and I thought it would be nice to try to start something," he later said.[10]

Taking a post at Berkeley was attractive also because he could postpone work for a year in order to stay on in Europe and continue studying mathematics, a field in which he thought he was still weak. The University of California would also let him teach each spring in Pasadena at the California Institute of Technology, better known as Cal Tech.

3

"I saw what the Depression was doing"

Before taking on his new career as a university teacher, Oppenheimer and his brother Frank enjoyed a holiday together at a ranch they had leased in the Upper Pecos Valley in Oppenheimer's beloved New Mexico. Katherine Page had christened their new home Perro Caliente, which was Spanish for "hot dog"—Robert Oppenheimer's first words when he learned he could lease the ranch.[1] The rough log cabin on the site had only primitive bathroom and cooking facilities, but the ranch became a regular holiday spot for the two brothers and their friends over the next few years.

In 1929, when Robert Oppenheimer arrived in California, the teeming beaches, the vast subdivisions, and the snarled freeways draped in smog were still far in the future. There wasn't even a Golden Gate Bridge across the mouth of San Francisco Bay. For Robert Oppenheimer to take a job at the University of California at Berkeley was something of a gamble, especially when he could have had a post at Harvard with its rich academic traditions and close ties to the universities of Europe. But the gamble paid off both for him and the university.

At twenty-five Oppenheimer was a poor lecturer, who raced through his notes at a fast clip, spoke in abstract prose, and punctuated his talks with several disturbing mannerisms. After one of his first lectures, a professor congratulated him by saying, "Well, Robert, I didn't understand a damn word!"

His students, mostly at the graduate level, found him intolerant of stupidity and impatient with those who seemed ignorant or arrogant. Some students even complained about him to the head of the physics department. But gradually, Oppenheimer began to slow down and to work harder on his delivery. Eventually, he became the favorite of an adoring group of young theoretical physicists, who imitated his walk, his manner of speaking, and even his chain smoking. They called him "Oppie," a version of the nickname "Opje" that he had picked up while studying physics in Europe.

Even so, taking notes in his lectures was never easy. One story was told about a student who questioned Oppenheimer about a particular equation he cited while gesturing at a blackboard. Oppenheimer said, "No, not that one, the one underneath."

"But there isn't one underneath," the student said.

"Not below," answered Oppenheimer, "underneath. I have written over it."

Glenn Seaborg, a chemistry student who went on to win the Nobel Prize, told of another problem: "I had one difficulty with Oppie that I imagine was common to all who sought his advice, that is, facing his tendency to answer your question even before you had fully stated it. In this respect, I recall taking great pains in formulating my questions to him in such a way that I could put the main thrust of my thoughts as early as possible into every sentence."[2]

Oppenheimer wasn't the only "star" in physics on campus at Berkeley. A year before his arrival another remarkable physicist, Ernest Orlando Lawrence, had been hired as an associate professor and had begun building the first in a series of atom smashers, or cyclotrons, machines that accelerated atomic particles to high energies and used them to bombard nuclei.

First Lawrence built an eleven-inch cyclotron, which required a two-ton magnet to make it work. But gradually, he had moved up to a sixty-inch cyclotron.

The two of them—Lawrence, the energetic experimentalist, and Oppenheimer, the intellectual theorist—formed an unusual but fruitful partnership. Lawrence and the experimentalists at Cal Tech would make discoveries about the atom, and Oppenheimer and his students would explain the theories behind them.

The two of them began to turn Berkeley into an international center for physics, and by the end of the 1930s budding physicists no longer felt compelled to go to Europe to study. They could go to Berkeley or Cal Tech to learn under Lawrence or Oppenheimer.

Gradually, Oppenheimer swung into a pleasant California life-style: teaching at Berkeley in the fall and at Cal Tech in the spring, visits to Perro Caliente in the summer. There were regular visits from his father; his mother died in 1931.

Oppenheimer's relations with students were not confined to the classroom. Sometimes he worked late with students and then continued the discussion at a dinner at Jack's, a fine restaurant in San Francisco, where he would pick up the bill. Sometimes the conversation that began with science would end with art, music, literature, or politics. Sometimes the group would take the night off and have a Mexican dinner in Oakland or go to a movie.

Although his university salary was small, Oppenheimer also had money from his family, and he willingly footed the bill for all. "The world of good food and good wines and gracious living was far from the experience of many of them," said one student, Robert Serber, who went on to become a distinguished university professor himself, "and Oppie was introducing them to an unfamiliar way of life. We acquired something of his tastes. We went to concerts together and listened to chamber music."

The only time they seemed to find his company objectionable was when he did the cooking. He had taught himself to make an Indonesian dish, *nasi goreng*, which he seasoned excessively with hot spices. The students called it "nasty gory."

Oppenheimer was not the typical physicist by any means. While at Berkeley he studied Sanskrit, an ancient language of India, privately with one of the professors so that he could read the *Bhagavad Gita*, a sacred Hindu poem about the god Krishna, in the original.

He claimed to know several languages: Spanish, German, French, Dutch, Italian, Greek, and Latin. Not everyone believed he was as proficient as he claimed to be, and some thought that he flaunted knowledge he did have. One colleague, Nobel Prize winner Emilio Segrè, an immigrant from Italy, said that on one occasion he arrived at Oppenheimer's home for dinner only to find Oppenheimer seated in an easy chair where he was reading the sonnets of the Italian writer Petrarch in the original Italian. Segrè was irritated and felt the performance was being put on for his benefit.

"I knew English better than he knew Italian and yet I would not have been ready to sit down in front of him to read the sonnets of Shakespeare, which were not any easier than Petrarch's," Segrè said.

His occasional arrogance gave a dark side to Oppenheimer's personality and aroused some resentment. There seemed to be no one among the great minds in physics in this century whom Oppenheimer was not afraid to interrupt or contradict. Once one of Oppenheimer's former professors from Göttingen, James Franck, the winner of a Nobel Prize in 1925, visited Berkeley to deliver a series of lectures, "The Fundamental

Meaning of Quantum Mechanics." Franck had been known as almost a saint in Germany, a man who was always warm and kindly to his students.

As part of his visit Franck attended a lecture by one of Oppenheimer's students and asked a question that seemed embarrassingly silly to others in the room. Oppenheimer spoke up: "I don't intend to deliver any lectures on the fundamental meaning of quantum mechanics, but the meaning of that question is a foolish one."

Students often suffered at his hands as well. Glenn Seaborg, for example, as a graduate student, had made a discovery along with a colleague of his. "We wrote it up and showed it to Ernest Lawrence to get his approval before sending it to the *American Physical Review* to be published," Seaborg said.[3]

Lawrence decided to confer first with Oppenheimer, who contended that he saw an error in the paper. So Lawrence insisted that the students hold it back until they had worked out the problem. Almost immediately after that, the same results were published in a French journal. "So then we published ours," Seaborg said, "but, of course, we were second."

Oppenheimer was known for his overwhelming intellect, his ability to grasp difficult problems easily, and yet he never came up with top-league solutions. He traveled through life in the company of Nobel Prize winners, yet he never won the prize himself. Nobel laureates respected his fine intellect, yet his work never matched their achievements. Often, according to his friends, he would be working diligently on some problem, on the track of solutions, and yet the final answers came from others. His good friend Isidor I. Rabi, himself a Nobel Prize winner, said that in a way Oppenheimer was "over-educated in those fields which lie outside the scientific tradition."

According to Rabi: "He was insufficiently confident of the power of the intellectual tools he already possessed and did not drive his thought to the very end because he felt instinctively that new ideas and new methods were necessary to go further than he and his students had already gone."[4]

"He was a dilettante," said another scientist. "He just would not take his coat off and really get stuck in. He'd got the ability certainly, but he hadn't got the staying power."[5]

That doesn't mean Oppenheimer never made any discoveries. In the 1930s he and one of his graduate students, Melba Phillips, studied the results of cyclotron experiments in which elements bombarded by the nuclei of an isotope of hydrogen became radioactive. They explained the process by which a bombarded nucleus was turned into a new radioactive atom. This explanation, known as the Oppenheimer–Phillips process, is still considered important in understanding nuclear reactions.

Oppenheimer also reported on the measurements of the absorption of cosmic rays by various materials. He used quantum mechanics to explain changes in the path and velocity of atomic particles or systems when they collide.

In spite of his shortcomings, his appeal drew others toward him. Physicist Robert Serber told of how he had received his Ph.D. working at the University of Wisconsin and was on his way to the East Coast in 1934 to study further at an eastern university. Along the way he stopped at the University of Michigan to spend a month at the summer session. Oppenheimer was there, and after hearing him lecture and talking to him a little, Serber changed direction and went out West to Berkeley to study.

Until the mid-1930s Oppenheimer seemed totally caught up in the world of physics and the university. He read widely in the classics, novels, and plays but never looked at magazines or newspapers. He had no telephone or radio and didn't learn about the 1929 stock market crash until six months after it occurred, when Ernest Lawrence happened to tell him about it.

The first time he voted was in the 1936 presidential election. In that year he became politically active in other ways, partly due to the influence of a young woman, Jean Tatlock, who was at Berkeley to study for a doctorate in psychology. Tall and slender, with dark hair and green eyes, Jean Tatlock attracted Oppenheimer with both her looks and her intelligence.

Although Tatlock was the daughter of a Berkeley professor known for his right-wing views, she was very involved with leftist groups. By the time she met Oppenheimer she had joined the Communist Party. Many intellectuals and liberals of the time had also joined the party or left-wing groups with close ties to Communism.

By then a number of political and social problems had intruded into Oppenheimer's secure academic life and disrupted his detachment from the outside world. He had become furious about the oppression of Jews in Germany. He had relatives there and arranged to bring them to the United States.

Financially secure himself, Oppenheimer also worried about the finances of others. "I saw what the Depression was doing to my students," he later said. "Often they could get no jobs or jobs which were wholly inadequate."[6] When his father died in 1937 and Oppenheimer came into an inheritance, he made a will leaving his money to the University of California for fellowships for graduate students.

Oppenheimer was also aroused about the Spanish civil war, in which the Communist Party was pitting its forces against the Fascists, who were headed by Franco and supported by Germany.

In the same year, 1936, Oppenheimer's brother Frank, a physics student, married Jacquenette Quann, a fellow University of California student. A few months after their marriage the couple joined the Communist Party.

Although Robert Oppenheimer never joined the Communist Party, these Communist friends and relatives deepened his associations with left-wing groups. These affiliations would later return to haunt him.

Within a year after meeting Jean Tatlock, Oppenheimer had become involved in such groups as the Friends of the Chinese People, the Western Council of the Consumers' Union, and the American Committee for Democracy and Intellectual Freedom. The last group had strong connections with the Communist Party.

He subscribed to the leftist *People's World*; he contributed to committees that helped the Spanish Loyalist cause. "I had never been to Spain; I knew a little of its literature; I knew nothing of its politics or contemporary problems," Oppenheimer said later in explaining all of this. "But like a great many other Americans, I was emotionally committed to the Loyalist cause. . . . The end of the war and the defeat of the Loyalists caused me great sorrow."[7]

Oppenheimer also helped found a teacher's union for faculty and teaching assistants at the university and for schoolteachers in the area. He was even elected recording secretary of the group. During this time he met a person who would play a major role in his future life—Haakon Chevalier, a member of the modern languages faculty at Berkeley who served as president of the teachers' union.

For three years Oppenheimer and Jean Tatlock had an on-again, off-again romance and at times considered themselves engaged to be married. Theirs was a stormy relationship, plagued by Jean's problems with depression. By 1939 they had broken up, but Oppenheimer maintained many of his ties and donations to leftist groups. This was strange in view of the fact that visitors to Russia at that time returned to tell of concentration camps and purge trials and Stalin's crackdown on personal freedom.

In 1939 Russia also signed a nonaggression pact with Nazi Germany, which shocked many who had faith that Stalin and the Communists would keep Hitler in check in Europe. Nationwide, many Communists resigned from the party. But it wasn't until two years later that Oppenheimer finally broke all his ties with left-wing groups.

While all this was going on politically, Oppenheimer had met and fallen in love with another woman, Katherine Puening Harrison, the wife of Stewart Harrison, an English doctor doing cancer research at Cal Tech.

Kitty, as she was usually called, had a confused past, including several attempts to get through college. Harrison was her third husband. Shortly after graduating from college, she had married for the first time, a marriage to a musician that lasted only a few months.

In the 1930s she had married Joe Dallet, a union organizer, a member of the Communist Party, and the son of a wealthy investment banker. Under his influence she sold copies of the *Daily Worker* on street corners, passed out leaflets at factories, and eventually joined the Communist Party herself. But she quickly became disillusioned with their life of poverty and hardship and left Dallet so she could return to school.

During their separation Dallet joined a large group of American volunteers who went to Spain to fight side by side with the Loyalist forces in the civil war. They reconciled, and she was on her way to meet him in Spain when she learned he had been killed. However stormy their marriage had been, his death devastated her.

She returned to school to study biology at the University of Pennsylvania and soon married Harrison, a man she had known since she was a teenager. But within a year she had filed for a divorce so that she could marry Robert Oppenheimer.

The speed of their romance and marriage shocked many of Oppenheimer's friends, and some of them felt that Kitty was a schemer and a manipulator, particularly after old friends began to be excluded from their social circle and new ones moved in. "If Kitty wanted anything, she would always get it," said Jackie Oppenheimer, Frank's wife.[8]

In 1941 Kitty gave birth to their first child, Peter, and soon the family moved into a new home on Eagle Hill in Berkeley.

"Nuclear transformations of an explosive character"

What happened next in Oppenheimer's life was the result of a long, complicated series of events, involving many other scientists and nations far away from his sheltered university life in California.

For many years physicists had not been restrained by national divisions or boundaries. In their realm of blackboards and laboratories and cyclotrons, information on discoveries about the atom passed freely from Rome to Copenhagen to Cambridge to Berkeley and back again, right up to the start of World War II. It was a world that judged people on their scientific knowledge and discoveries rather than on their nationality or religion. Physicists believed that pure science should not be involved with politics or government.

But more and more they found the outside world impossible to ignore as Hitler came to power in Germany. As Hitler's conquests spread, those living and working in the academic world of Europe teetered on the brink of a cliff. Many scientists, particularly those of Jewish ancestry, fled from country to country. Some ended up as refugees in the United States, where universities, hungry to learn more about their research, welcomed them with open arms.

Despite what was happening, physicists' discoveries about the atom in the 1930s roared ahead. First, in 1931 Sir John Cockcroft and Ernest T. Walton, working for Rutherford in England, split a lithium atom with a beam of protons in the world's first particle accelerator. Then, in 1932 James Chadwick, also at Cambridge, discovered the neutron, one of the elementary atomic particles that can be used to penetrate and split atoms.

Two years later the Joliot-Curies of France discovered artificial radioactivity. They bombarded boron, aluminum, and magnesium with alpha particles and found that after the bombardment stopped, radiation continued.

For the first time physicists had a hint of the awful power of the atom. When the Joliot-Curies later accepted their Nobel Prize in Stockholm for their discovery, Frederic Joliot-Curie told the audience: "We are justified in reflecting that scientists who can construct and demolish elements at will may also be capable of causing nuclear transformations of an explosive character. . . ."[1]

That idea—that the atom's energy might be turned into a bomb—had already occurred to Leo Szilard, a young Hungarian physicist who, like many scientists of Europe, had become a refugee and had finally ended up in the United States. His experiences with Hitler and his fears about atomic power led him in 1935 to approach several physicists and ask them if it wouldn't be a good idea to refrain from publishing the results of atomic research so that they wouldn't fall into the wrong hands.

At first other scientists found the proposal laughable. After all, they had only begun their conquest of the atom. At that point they hadn't yet discovered the concept of nuclear fission.

They pressed on with their work. In Rome, Enrico Fermi

and his associates bombarded the heaviest metal, uranium, with neutrons and found what they believed was a new element or perhaps several new ones.

Then, in 1938 two physicists in Hitler's Germany, Otto Hahn and Fritz Strassmann, again bombarded uranium with neutrons and discovered that they had divided the uranium atom into two almost equal parts of radioactive barium.

They didn't know what they had discovered, but the answer was clear to Lise Meitner, a former collaborator of Hahn's. Meitner, who had fled Germany for Sweden, and her nephew, Otto Frisch, published the correct interpretation of the results and for the first time used the term *nuclear fission* to describe the division of a heavy atomic nucleus into two almost equal parts.

After the start of World War II, other scientists began wondering if Hitler would use these atomic discoveries, many of them known to German scientists, to create a weapon to use against the rest of the world.

Szilard and some friends—Eugene Wigner, Edward Teller, and Victor Weisskopf, all refugees from Hitler's Europe—wanted to convince the American government of the importance of the new atomic research in the making of weapons.

No one in Washington seemed interested, not even after an important meeting of physicists in the nation's capital in 1939. At that session the prominent Danish physicist Niels Bohr announced that a bomb containing a tiny amount of uranium 235 bombarded by neutrons could set off an explosion big enough to blow up an entire laboratory and most of the surrounding town.[2]

What Szilard's group didn't know was that the Germans had made only a little progress at that time. Some German scientists later claimed that they tried to avoid working with Hitler's war machine or that they only pretended to do so. At the same time, Germany, strapped by the war effort, was unable to get together the men and materials needed for the massive undertaking.

Unaware of all that, Szilard approached the physicist Albert Einstein, who had left Europe to take a post at Princeton University in the United States. Szilard proposed that Einstein write to President Franklin Roosevelt to ask the United States to fund stepped-up atomic research.

Einstein, known for his antiwar feelings, later regretted his role in the matter and claimed he had assumed that the United States would never use such a bomb except for self-defense against a similar weapon.

Although Roosevelt was convinced of the need to move ahead with the project, progress was slow for two years. A Presidential Committee on Uranium was set up to coordinate research on developing isotopes that could be used in a bomb and achieving the kind of sustained chain reaction needed for a bomb. But only three hundred thousand dollars was allocated by the government to sixteen research groups. And the need for secrecy, for fear that the Germans might find out about the project, meant the various scientific groups had to work separately without sharing knowledge and problems.

At long last, in 1942 the project was reorganized and put under the control of the Army Corps of Engineers. For the first time a sense of urgency and purpose was put into the project, which became known as Manhattan Engineer District, after the area in which it was located. It was part of the newly set up Office of Scientific Research and Development headed by Vannevar Bush and James B. Conant. The word *Manhattan* was chosen because New York was the first headquarters for the district.

One of the first tasks of the physicists and chemists brought into the project was to decide which methods to use to separate material for an atomic bomb. Uranium 235 was one isotope of uranium that scientists believed could be used to make a bomb. Plutonium, another rare element, which could be produced only by laboratory methods, was also believed to be useful in making bombs.

Three methods were being considered, all difficult to set up and all producing only minute quantities of the necessary isotope: gaseous diffusion, thermal diffusion, and the electromagnetic process, developed by Oppenheimer's friend at the university, Ernest O. Lawrence.

Lawrence began working on converting his latest cyclotron into a machine that could remove the precious uranium 235 isotope from uranium ore. To help him in analyzing his data he called on Robert Oppenheimer.

This was Oppenheimer's first involvement with the nuclear project, but soon he was attending many meetings on the bomb. On October 21, 1941, he went to a conference at the General Electric Laboratories in Schenectady, New York, where he drafted the calculations for how the bomb would work.

The explosive chain reaction would be set off by one neutron hitting an atom of uranium 235. This atom would split, producing two barium atoms and three more neutrons plus energy. The freed neutrons would then travel off to split other atoms.

Oppenheimer also calculated the size of the piece of uranium needed to produce the bomb—one hundred kilograms. This was called the critical mass. Anything smaller would not provide enough collisions of neutrons and atoms to cause an explosion.

Basically, a fifty-kilogram "subcritical" piece of uranium 235 had to be brought together with another fifty-kilogram subcritical piece in order to produce an explosion.[3]

Oppenheimer's work was so valuable to the fledgling groups of scientists that Arthur Holly Compton, a professor at the University of Chicago and leader of the bomb project, soon asked him to work full-time on the project. By May 1942 Oppenheimer was supervising the discussion of how the bomb mechanism would be constructed. This was only six months after he had attended his last Spanish War Veterans meeting and a short time after he finally stopped making payments to Communist Party charities. One of the first problems that Oppenheimer set to work on was confirmation of his own calculations about the critical mass needed for the uranium bomb. Throughout the summer of 1942 a small group of scientists met on the Berkeley campus in the attic rooms of Le Conte Hall, a large science building where Oppenheimer had his office. Among those attending the meetings were Edward Teller, Emil Konopinski, Felix Bloch, and three of Oppenheimer's former students: Stanley Frankel, Eldred Nelson, and Robert Serber. Since they were in the center of a bustling university campus, they adopted security arrangements. The windows were covered with wire mesh, and the door was fitted with a special lock with a single key that only Oppenheimer could use.

At their meetings the scientists talked about how the bomb would look and what its basic size would be. They saw it as being a heavy metal shell containing a sphere of uranium before explosion. When the uranium mass became critical and the reaction began, the metal shell would contain the explosion for a few milliseconds and reflect back escaping neutrons into the fissioning uranium metal.[4]

Other ideas also came up at these sessions. One was a proposal for a bomb that could be five times bigger than the fission bomb and that would cost far less. Such a bomb would be powered by fusion of light nuclei such as those of hydrogen. Edward Teller in particular was interested in this idea and repeatedly urged the others to consider working on what he called the "super." It could be made from deuterium gas, a heavy form of hydrogen that would produce five times as much energy as a fission reaction in uranium. Deuterium is also cheaper and easier to obtain than uranium.

Teller pushed hard for further research on the device but

then came up with another theory that shocked the little group. He suggested that any atomic explosion might trigger an uncontrolled reaction in the atmosphere. A bomb, he suggested, might create enough heat to set the earth's atmosphere on fire.

Oppenheimer called an immediate halt to the discussions until Teller's results could be checked. The German refugee scientist Hans Bethe was assigned to go through Teller's calculations, and Oppenheimer sought out his immediate superior, Arthur Compton.

Oppenheimer speeded by train to Michigan where Compton was on vacation at a lake cottage. Compton was horrified and urged the group to study the matter further.

Bethe determined that Teller's calculations did not allow for heat losses due to radiation. He also said it seemed technologically impossible to develop the kind of fusion bomb that Teller was talking about.

Some have theorized that the damper that was put on the H-bomb, or fusion bomb, at this point was the seed of future hostility between Teller and Oppenheimer. But Teller says differently: "The hydrogen bomb was the main topic . . . and there was no difference of opinion about the propriety of discussing the subject."[5]

5

"He is absolutely essential to the project"

In October 1942 a burly brigadier general with dark brown hair and mustache and a uniform that bulged at his plump waistline got off a train in San Francisco to shake Ernest Lawrence's hand. The general was Leslie R. Groves, the newly named chief of the Manhattan Project, the most secret undertaking of World War II.

Groves had just spent several days traveling across the country to various universities in search of the best method for separating the fissionable uranium 235 isotope from the uranium 238 isotope. The winning method was going to be incorporated into a massive plant in Tennessee that would produce purified uranium.

But at each stop Groves was disappointed at the progress being made. In Pittsburgh he had visited the Westinghouse Research Laboratories, where a centrifuge process had been developed. Big cylinder drums were spun at dizzying speeds in order to separate the U-235 from the heavier U-238. But so far very little had been accomplished, and to Groves the group of people working there seemed to be going at too relaxed a pace. He recommended to the government that the centrifuge process be dropped.

At Columbia University in New York, he looked at the gaseous diffusion process that called for turning uranium 238 into uranium hexafluoride, a gas, and forcing it through a filter made up of microscopic holes. It was believed that the lighter molecules containing uranium 235 would move through the filter more quickly than the heavier molecules containing uranium 238, and they could thus be separated from each other. But the problem was that uranium hexafluoride is so corrosive it eats up any pipe, filter, or pump. The biggest obstacle for the Columbia group was finding a metal alloy to use in the filter.

At the University of Chicago, scientists, led by Nobel Prize winner and Italian refugee Enrico Fermi, were trying to build an atomic pile that would allow them to produce plutonium, another possible element that could be used in a bomb. Groves had also been upset there by the lack of precise estimates that the scientists could give him about how much material was actually needed for a bomb.

Last of all he went to California to see Lawrence in Berkeley. Lawrence took Groves on a tour of his "calutron"—*calu* after the University of California and *tron* from cyclotron. Inside a warehouse-size building high in the hills above Berkeley and San Francisco Bay, Lawrence had built a giant machine that accelerated atoms of uranium gas through a circular chamber to a speed of many thousands of miles per second. As they reached this speed, they entered the field of a 184-inch magnet. By the pull of magnetic force the atoms were curved into circular paths. The lighter uranium 235 atoms were bent into a different path from that of the heavier uranium 238 atoms. The lighter atoms would go farther than the others because air resistance is different depending on size. At the end of the arc were two containers: one to catch heavier atoms, one to catch the lighter atoms. Groves was impressed with Lawrence's optimism and energy. The only problem was that the machine had never been run for more than ten to fifteen minutes, and as yet Lawrence had not separated any of the 235 from the 238.

Groves had now traveled thousands of miles to meet with the nation's top physicists and had yet to meet anyone collecting significant amounts of uranium to make a bomb. His next meeting was with Robert Oppenheimer, who was in charge of designing the bomb. The two of them seemed as unlike in personality as possible. On the one hand, there was the frail Oppenheimer, New York–born liberal and intellectual, son of a German immigrant father. On the other, there was the robust Groves, West Point graduate and the son of a Presbyterian army chaplain. He had been raised largely in the West and was committed to a military life.

Records are scarce on what happened at that first meeting of the two men, yet for some reason Groves was impressed with Oppenheimer and with how he handled his small group of scientists that summer. Oppenheimer had always been someone who could grasp the overview of a complicated problem, and his experiences with his devoted students showed that the shy youth had grown into a master at attracting and managing people.

All of this must have become clear to Groves very quickly because he next arranged for Oppenheimer to fly to Chicago and then to ride with him and two of his associates on the Twentieth Century Limited, the famous passenger train, as they went on to New York. As they rode along, Oppenheimer talked about his distress over the compartmentalization of the bomb project. The government felt, for example, that there was no need for people at the University of Chicago to know about gaseous diffusion. Nor should Lawrence's group at Berkeley know what was happening with Fermi's group in Chicago.

All across the country different groups were working on

different projects, and some were duplicating another group's efforts. Some of them had solved problems that other groups were still working on. There was no sharing of information. Part of that was due to the need for secrecy and security on the project, but some of it was also due to the fact that the work was so spread out.

Groves and Oppenheimer began discussing the possibility of bringing all of the scientists together in one weapons laboratory, where security could be rigidly enforced and where the various parts of the project could be meshed together. Once a bomb was prepared, an isolated proving ground would also be necessary.

Chicago was considered as a possibility, but of course security would be difficult to maintain in a large city. Oak Ridge, Tennessee, where a factory was being built to produce fissionable material for the bomb, was also proposed. But Oppenheimer and others didn't like the idea of having a scientific group attached to a production facility.

The ideal, Groves decided, would be a laboratory located in the inland wilderness of the United States. The search soon narrowed to the southern Rockies and five possible sites across a two-hundred-mile area from northern New Mexico to Las Vegas. Eventually, the choices were narrowed down to two places in the Jemez Mountain Range of northern New Mexico—Jemez Springs and the Los Alamos Ranch School, a private boys' academy.

In mid-November 1942 Oppenheimer, who as yet didn't know what his role would be at the weapons laboratory, inspected the two sites with Groves. Jemez Springs, located in a deep canyon, was quickly ruled out. It seemed too restricted for laboratories and housing, and boundary fences on the steep rock walls couldn't be patrolled.

So the group got into their cars and rode to the Los Alamos Ranch School, a spot that Oppenheimer had visited before because it was close to his ranch, Perro Caliente. Los Alamos was a high plateau, part of a mountain range created by an ancient and extinct volcano. At its lower levels the plateau was covered with piñons, juniper, and many varieties of scrub. On upper levels it supported ponderosa pine, fir, spruce, oak, and aspen.

It was a sunny site, something like a mountain resort, about sixteen to eighteen miles away from the nearest town. Off in the distance could be seen the Sangre de Cristo (Blood of Christ) Mountains. The Spaniards had given the mountains that name after watching the sun turn the snow on the peaks to a glowing red.

One additional factor made the site desirable for a laboratory. On the plateau was the Los Alamos Ranch School, a boarding school for boys that had an enrollment of about forty-five. The school buildings, it was estimated, could provide housing for about thirty scientists. Only one poor road led to Santa Fe, but Groves felt it could easily be improved. The government began condemnation proceedings in December 1942, and by mid-February the boys had left the school for good. The choice pleased Oppenheimer who had long loved New Mexico.

After Groves had picked a location for the bomb laboratory, his next decision was to choose a leader for that laboratory. He needed someone brilliant, of course, and someone with prestige, who could attract the best people to work at the laboratory.

His next thought was to appoint Ernest Lawrence head of the laboratory, partly because he was a Nobel Prize winner but also because Groves had been impressed by Lawrence's enthusiasm and determination that he would get the job done regardless of the obstacles ahead. But he had to keep Lawrence in place at the University of California, where he could work on the electromagnetic separation process that was going to be used at the Tennessee uranium-production plant. Other scientists were also considered. For example, Fermi was a possibility because of his high standing and brilliance. But he was a recent refugee to the United States, and it would be unlikely that U.S. officials would want to commit such a top-secret project to the leadership of someone who was foreign-born.

At that point Groves decided that Oppenheimer was the most likely choice even though Oppenheimer lacked a number of key characteristics. He was not a Nobel Prize winner; he was a theoretical physicist, not an experimental thinker; he had never managed or run such a vast operation before. In addition, several people whom Groves consulted, including Lawrence, were not sure that Oppenheimer could handle such a project.

On the other hand, Oppenheimer had been educated in both the United States and Europe. He held professorships at two California universities and had earned a reputation as an outstanding teacher who had cultivated many brilliant students who now were leading teachers themselves. He had had more than forty articles and notes published in the *Physical Review*. He understood scientists and was an excellent thinker and speaker.

There was one other catch about the choice of Oppenheimer as director—his previous associations with Communist-backed organizations. The FBI contacted Groves and warned him about Oppenheimer's background. "As always in security matters of such importance, I had read all the available evidence," Groves later said. "I did not depend upon the conclusion of the security officers."[1]

The FBI had assembled an ever-growing file on Oppenheimer. On the one hand, there was the fact that his wife, his brother, and his sister-in-law had once been members of the Communist Party. There was also evidence from surveillance of Communists in California that some members of the party knew about the weapons project and were interested in Oppenheimer's role in the project, although there is no evidence that Oppenheimer knew anything about their interest at that point.[2]

After reviewing the files, Groves decided that Oppenheimer's importance to the building of an atomic bomb far outweighed any questions about his past. After all, there had been many Americans who had supported the Spanish Communists in the war against Franco, and furthermore in the 1940s Russia was our ally against Hitler, not our enemy.

The questions about Oppenheimer's background indicated that he could not receive security clearance in the usual way. Groves was personally forced to order that he be given clearance. Groves wrote to his superiors: "He [Oppenheimer] is absolutely essential to the project."[3] Oppenheimer's new role as head of Los Alamos had begun.

6

"A hero who never appeared to be one"

Imagine taking a job in a faraway desert laboratory, where you would live and work in rough, makeshift buildings heated by wood stoves. You couldn't tell any of your friends or relatives where you had gone or what you were doing. Because of tight security, letters and phone calls to the outside world would probably be censored, and you could seldom leave your new home. When you did leave, you'd have to travel by rough, winding mountain roads to the nearest city. You would be expected to work long hours of overtime on a highly secret project that seemed unlikely to end in success. If you were married, you could take your family along. If not, you couldn't take any friend or relative with you.

That was part of what Oppenheimer had to offer to the scientists he wanted to recruit for Los Alamos. Of course, there were advantages as well—the beautiful mountain scenery and the chance to put unlimited funds and manpower into scientific discoveries that would change the world.

Originally, Oppenheimer had proposed a laboratory of

thirty scientists. Quickly, he revised his estimates to one hundred and then to fifteen hundred. Over the next few months, while still living in Berkeley, Oppenheimer drew up plans for what Los Alamos would be like and began recruiting a staff. He wrote to many of his prospects, but he also traveled from university to university to contact the best scientists personally. One of his main jobs was to convince them that the project that had so long been stuck in a quagmire, unable to make any progress, would finally move ahead.

Many of those who signed on had worked with Oppenheimer at the University of California and were swayed by his magnetic personality. The university had been chosen to run the new laboratory for the Manhattan Engineer District of the army.

But others from throughout the country came, spurred on by the vision that Oppenheimer gave them of the race that the United States was in to develop an atom bomb before the Germans did. He now poured into the laboratory project the same fervor that he had once poured into the Spanish civil war and political crusades.

The Los Alamos roster was rich with top scientists, many of them Nobel Prize winners: Enrico Fermi, Emilio Segrè, Niels Bohr, I. I. Rabi, Hans Bethe, John von Neumann, Edward Teller, George Kistiakowsky, Otto Frisch, and Richard Feynmann.

Although these physicists knew what their task would be at Los Alamos, what was called Project Y remained a mystery to dozens of other administrators and secretaries and technicians until their arrival. "The notion of disappearing into the desert for an indeterminate period and under quasi-military auspices disturbed a good many scientists and the families of many more," Oppenheimer said later.[1]

Because of the need for secrecy, Groves proposed making Los Alamos a military base and giving all of the scientists army ranks. To the surprise of many colleagues, Oppenheimer at first agreed and began steps toward enrolling as a lieutenant colonel. But the scientists soon objected, particularly those who had fled the increasing militarism in Europe. They felt that military management would be too rigid to allow for the free thought needed in a laboratory.

Quickly, Oppenheimer abandoned this idea out of fear that it might scare off the physicists he wanted to recruit. Groves agreed as well that the scientists would be out of character in uniform.

Meanwhile, some three thousand workers, who had no idea what they were building, threw up ramshackle wooden houses and barracks at Los Alamos, and bulldozers cut out streets and roads. School buildings were remodeled, and the head teachers' houses became homes for the top project administrators.

Although recruitment took Oppenheimer three months, scientists began arriving at Los Alamos while walls were still going up; these early arrivals were farmed out to local ranches. Every day, until housing was ready, staff members had to travel to the site over the bumpy, narrow road. One noisy Forest Service telephone line was the only communication with the project office in Santa Fe.

Four-family houses, government trailers, and prefabricated buildings created an instant city on the once windswept, empty plateau. Squat military huts stretched for blocks along unpaved, dusty streets that had turned into a forest of chimneys and telephone poles.

In spite of the hardworking carpenters and plumbers, there were never as many apartments and huts and trailers as there were families. Water was as precious as gasoline had become under wartime rationing. One wooden water tank served the entire project. When the gauge on the outside was dangerously low, baths were forbidden.

Soon special equipment began to arrive: generators, an accelerator, a cyclotron. Oppenheimer moved to Los Alamos in March 1943, and amid the chaos he managed to create organization and a sense of purpose. One of those he recruited was Dorothy McKibbin, a Santa Fe widow, hired to take charge of the new laboratory's Santa Fe office. She had been hesitant to take the job, although it promised more money than the bank job she already had. But when she met Oppenheimer, his determination and intensity impressed her so that she accepted the offer.

For the next few years she gave a warm welcome to hundreds of scientists and their family members who stopped off at her office on East Palace Street. Mrs. McKibbin arranged transportation and housing for them and gave them their passes to Los Alamos.

Although Oppenheimer's job was mainly supposed to be a scientific task, he soon found himself making decisions on housing, security, salaries, buying supplies, running the business office, building and maintaining houses and offices. All of this in spite of the fact that he had never even served as chairman of a physics department.

Although he had previously slept late in the mornings and never lectured before eleven, he began to rise at daybreak and was always at his desk before 8 A.M. He continued to work late as he had before.

While the buildings were being constructed, Oppenheimer gave up his impeccably tailored expensive suits for a pair of blue jeans and a checked shirt. These casual clothes made it easier to scramble over the building sites. Where once he had been known for his abruptness and tendency toward sarcasm, he tempered his sharpness and became known for his skillful handling of difficult and sometimes embarrassing situations.

Norris Bradbury, who went to Los Alamos to work in the explosives division, recalls the great contrast he saw between Oppenheimer the University of California teacher and Oppenheimer the leader of the laboratory.

"I was surprised to see him as director," Bradbury said.

"I wouldn't have thought him interested or capable of doing it, but he was excellent. He understood everything that was going on, and he became very much at ease with people, much more so than he had been as a teacher."[2]

Oppenheimer's close friend, Isidor I. Rabi, who was a consultant at Los Alamos but not on the staff, said he believed that General Groves showed tremendous genius and insight in choosing Oppenheimer to direct Los Alamos. "Running the laboratory was a complicated, difficult thing, dealing with a lot of prima donnas who were living under primitive conditions."[3]

"He really blossomed in Los Alamos as a leader," said Hans Bethe. "It was really the thing for which he was made— to have a big laboratory of very high-grade scientists and to be the leader of that group."[4]

Even those who clashed with Oppenheimer at times conceded that he put a spirit and soul into Los Alamos that made the laboratory unique. "He was incredibly quick and perceptive in understanding human as well as technical problems," said Edward Teller. "Of the more than ten thousand people who eventually came to work at Los Alamos, Oppie knew several hundred intimately. He knew their relationships to each other. He knew what made them tick. He knew how to organize, cajole, humor, soothe feelings—how to lead powerfully without seeming to do so. He was an exemplar of dedication, a hero who never appeared to be one or lost his humaness. Disappointing him carried with it a sense of wrongdoing. Los Alamos' success grew out of the brilliance, enthusiasm and charisma with which Oppenheimer led it."[5]

With the power he was given, Oppenheimer could have become a dictator. Instead, according to Hans Bethe, he was more like a good host who senses his guests' needs before they express them.

One reason behind his management success was that he had organized the laboratory in a democratic way. Of course, there were division leaders and group heads, but each week there were three separate assemblies where ideas could be exchanged and problems could be put on the table for discussion and solutions. A governing board of division leaders would meet to discuss policies. A coordinating council of the fifty group leaders also met each week. For Los Alamos at large, there were also weekly colloquiums open to all scientists who had bachelor's degrees. Although General Groves still fretted over whether too much information was being shared among the various groups, Oppenheimer continued to fight for the free interchange of ideas.

Oppenheimer was a genius at keeping in touch with the technical problems facing various groups at the laboratory and filed them in his head. He would often drop in unannounced at meetings. One scientist recalled a time when the laboratory director joined a metallurgy session where the group was arguing over what kind of container to use in melting plutonium. It wasn't exactly Oppenheimer's field at all. But after listening a while, he summed up the facts so clearly that although he didn't give the right answer himself, group members were immediately able to decide what they wanted to do.[6]

Within just a few days after they arrived at Los Alamos, the physicists began debating how they would put the bomb together—what they called the mechanism for the bomb. By that time it had been determined that the bomb could be made using either uranium 235 or the newly found element plutonium. The only catch was that Groves and his crews of scientists around the country had yet to produce enough of either substance in purified form to make a bomb. That hadn't stopped Groves from pressing ahead. Already under construction were massive factories at Oak Ridge, Tennessee, where workers would use the electromagnetic process developed by Ernest Lawrence and the gaseous diffusion process to try to come up with sufficient material for a bomb.

At Hanford, Washington, another huge plant, employing thousands of workers, would be built to purify plutonium.

Whether these plants would succeed was as debatable as whether Germany already had a bomb. In fact, in April 1943 the scientific world wasn't completely sure that plutonium even existed as a separate element.

The only fact that the scientists at Los Alamos were fairly confident about was that three times as much uranium 235 as plutonium would be needed to make a bomb—making plutonium a more attractive choice.

The bomb mechanism discussed first at Los Alamos was the gun method, a type of bomb already familiar to warfare experts. What was needed was a way of bringing the subcritical pieces of fissionable material together very quickly to trigger a chain reaction that would end in an explosion. The gun method seemed to be the answer.

Inside a bomb casing an artillery gun would fire a subcritical piece of uranium or fissionable material into another subcritical sphere of uranium. When the two pieces of uranium met, they would exceed the critical mass, and the nuclear explosion would take place.

One problem the scientists had to work on was ensuring that the two subcritical pieces were brought together quickly enough. Otherwise, stray neutrons might begin a reaction that would blow the bomb itself apart without creating a major explosion.

Then a young physicist, Seth Neddermeyer from the National Bureau of Standards, proposed a different method of building the bomb. His idea was to use an implosion method. A slightly subcritical mass of fissionable material would be shaped into a hollow sphere and surrounded by explosives. When these explosives were detonated, they would compress the sphere and increase the density of the fissionable material. The solid sphere thus produced would exceed the critical mass stage, and a nuclear explosion would take place.

Other scientists were skeptical. The main problem, they pointed out, would be the difficulty in creating an even and symmetrical shock wave to bear down on the sphere. If the shock waves were uneven, the sphere might be blown apart before it became critical.

Despite these questions Oppenheimer allowed Neddermeyer to work on the implosion method. Several months later this move proved to have been a wise one, when the gun method was found unsuitable for plutonium bombs. The plutonium produced at Oak Ridge and Hanford had a strong tendency toward spontaneous fission, releasing neutrons on its own. Assembly by the gun method would be too slow to prevent the bomb from blowing apart before a nuclear explosion took place. The implosion method would be the only way to put together a bomb using plutonium.

As Oppenheimer resolved one crisis after another during the early months at Los Alamos, he failed to solve one personnel problem successfully. As a result, he alienated someone with whom he would clash years later.

His difficulties were with Edward Teller, the Hungarian scientist whom Oppenheimer had worked with the summer before in Berkeley and whom Oppenheimer invited to come to Los Alamos. The two actually had many personality traits in common. Both had been outstanding students with many interests beyond the scientific world. Like Oppenheimer, Teller loved poetry, literature, and philosophical speculation. They were both strong, self-confident men, brilliant theorists who were often intolerant of stupidity and ignorance.

But almost from the first they failed to find a basis for friendship. Teller had come to Los Alamos under the mistaken impression that he would work on his proposal for the super, or hydrogen bomb, a weapon that would make use of a violent fusion reaction among molecules in deuterium. He grew upset because he was assigned to work under Hans Bethe, the head of the Theoretical Division at Los Alamos. According to Bethe, Teller worked on laboratory problems but in a "disinterested" way.[7]

Bethe came to accept Teller's detachment until work speeded up on the implosion method. At that point he asked Teller to develop a theory of implosion hydrodynamics, and Teller refused, according to Bethe. Teller flatly denied refusing but said later that he and Bethe "did not work well together."

Eventually, Oppenheimer moved Teller to a separate group where he could spend time working on the super. But the change may have come too late for the relationship between the two men. From that time on, the gulf between Oppenheimer and Teller began to grow, until one day it would be as vast as one of New Mexico's valleys.

7

"A question of past loyalties"

Although Oppenheimer had been put in charge of one of the most top-secret projects of World War II, he was still considered a security risk by the security officers for the Manhattan Project because of his past associations with Communists and Communist groups.

It's true, of course, that during World War II Communist Russia was considered the ally of the United States, whereas Germany and Japan were considered enemies. In spite of this, many people in the U.S. government didn't want to share secrets with Russia, particularly not the technology of the atom bomb, which would cost the United States hundreds of millions of dollars and the effort of tens of thousands of workers.

Among the officers at Los Alamos who were suspicious of Oppenheimer was Colonel John Lansdale, a lawyer who was an aide to General Groves on security matters. Lansdale was assigned to investigate possible Communist infiltration in Berkeley's Radiation Laboratory and thus uncovered some of

Oppenheimer's past political activities. Colonel Boris Pash, chief of counterintelligence for the Ninth Army Corps on the West Coast, the son of Russian immigrant parents who had a deep dislike for communism, also was apprehensive about Oppenheimer's loyalty.

Another officer who spent many hours observing and investigating Oppenheimer was Major Peer de Silva, chief of security at Los Alamos, who wrote many memos to his superiors outlining what he felt were questionable activities on Oppenheimer's part, although most of it was based on Oppenheimer's recruitment of liberal-minded scientists to work at the laboratory.

In fact, one of those who came to the laboratory was a German emigré, Klaus Fuchs, an atom researcher who did indeed pass on information about the bomb to the Russians. This espionage, however, was not discovered until several years after World War II. Oppenheimer denied any knowledge of what Fuchs was doing, and in fact, no connection was ever found between them.

At Los Alamos, Oppenheimer's every move was monitored. His mail was inspected, his phone and office were bugged, and a security officer was assigned to serve as his driver and bodyguard. As if this was not enough, these security men began a long series of interrogations and interviews, some with Oppenheimer, some with his wife, who was still under suspicion because of her former husband, Joe Dallet, the Communist who had died fighting in Spain. Oppenheimer broke off his ties to leftist groups in December 1942, but old friends from the past continued to reach out to him.

During the early months that Oppenheimer was associated with Los Alamos, one event in particular occurred that he would be questioned about many times in his life. Sometime in February 1943 Oppenheimer and his wife held a dinner party at their home in Berkeley for two old friends: Haakon Chevalier, professor of romance languages at Berkeley, who belonged to many of the same left-wing groups Oppenheimer once did, and Chevalier's wife.

At some point that evening Oppenheimer and Chevalier went into the kitchen alone, and Chevalier brought up a conversation he had had with a British scientist, George Eltenton, working for the Shell Oil Company in Berkeley. Eltenton had indicated that he had a means of sending scientific or technical data to the Soviet government.

Both Chevalier and Oppenheimer would say later that Oppenheimer refused flatly to be involved. Chevalier would claim later that he told Oppenheimer about Eltenton only because he wanted him to be aware of the situation, not because he was seeking information. What hurt Oppenheimer about the incident was not that it occurred or what he said but that he waited several months to report the incident to security officers and then gave differing versions of what had happened.

Another event occurred in June 1943 that was observed by security officers. By then Oppenheimer was living at Los Alamos, but he traveled back to Berkeley on a recruitment trip. Unknown to him, his travel was fully covered by agents assigned to watch him. In Berkeley he got word that his old girlfriend, Jean Tatlock, the Communist Party member, wanted to see him. Oppenheimer spent the night at her house, much of the time talking about Jean's personal problems. The next morning Tatlock drove Oppenheimer to the airport. It was the last time he would see her. Seven months later she killed herself with an overdose of sleeping pills. Although her relationship with Oppenheimer had been a stormy one, when he heard of her death he was shaken by the news.

At one point while investigating Oppenheimer, Colonel Boris Pash, who had been looking into alleged attempts by Communists to infiltrate the Berkeley Radiation Laboratory, recommended that Oppenheimer be removed from the Los

Alamos Laboratory because he might still be secretly affiliated with the Communist Party.

Another concern of security officers was a former student of Oppenheimer's, Giovanni Rossi Lomanitz, who had outspoken left-wing political views. Among other activities Lomanitz had helped organize the left-leaning Federation of Architects, Engineers, Chemists and Technicians in Berkeley. For a while security officers thought that Lomanitz also was involved in setting up a Soviet "cell" at Berkeley.

After Oppenheimer left Berkeley for Los Alamos, Ernest Lawrence thought so well of Lomanitz, who was only twenty-one at the time, that he asked the younger man to become a group head at the Radiation Laboratory. But within a week Lomanitz was told his selective service deferment had been canceled and he was going to be drafted. It was as if someone was trying to keep him from getting further involved in the Manhattan Project.

Lomanitz called Oppenheimer in New Mexico for help, and Oppenheimer sent a telegram to Lansdale urging that Lomanitz be kept at Berkeley. Oppenheimer interceded several more times for Lomanitz, but it was no use.

At the end of August, Oppenheimer visited Berkeley again and stopped off to see the campus security officer, Lieutenant Johnson, to ask if it would be all right to talk to Lomanitz, who was still on campus. Johnson said it would be all right but that he considered Lomanitz to be dangerous. At that point, without being asked, Oppenheimer volunteered some information that would cause him frequent problems for many years of his life.

He told Johnson that the security office should zero in on George Eltenton, the Shell engineer, who belonged to the scientific union that Lomanitz had helped organize. Oppenheimer also said that physicists had learned that Eltenton could supply information to the Soviets via their consulate in the Bay Area. Although this was basically the information that Chevalier had given him, Oppenheimer did not mention Chevalier's name or the incident at the dinner party.

That bit of information shook security officers attached to the Manhattan Project like a sonic boom. It wasn't that they hadn't heard about Eltenton before. He was already under suspicion. The problem was that never before had Eltenton been linked to Oppenheimer.

Oppenheimer was called back to Johnson's office the next day to meet with Johnson and Colonel Pash. Unknown to Oppenheimer, their conversation was taped by a hidden microphone and recorder. The two officers questioned Oppenheimer about the information he had given the day before. For reasons that Oppenheimer was never able to explain very well, he began to tell a complicated story about Eltenton. Again he did not name Chevalier.

Oppenheimer said he knew of two or three cases in which a nameless person had approached men at Los Alamos. Eltenton did not contact these scientists, he said; another party, a member of the Berkeley faculty, had done so. The faculty member had indicated that Eltenton could pass on information to the Soviets.

Oppenheimer said he did not view these incidents as attempts at treason. It was merely a case of someone who supported Soviet Russia and felt that the United States should share scientific information with its ally.

Pash wanted to know who the nameless person was, but Oppenheimer refused to identify him. "I think it would be a mistake," Oppenheimer said. "That is, I think I have told you where the initiative came from. To go any further would involve people who ought not to be involved in this."[1]

Pash believed that Oppenheimer was holding back information and had volunteered the story about Eltenton to divert investigators because he thought that his association with Lomanitz might have thrown suspicion on him.

By now Oppenheimer must have wished that he had

never mentioned Eltenton because the security officers would not stop asking about him. Next Oppenheimer was interviewed in Washington by Lansdale, Groves's aide, who also pressured Oppenheimer to tell who had contacted physicists about sharing information with the Soviets. During a two-hour conversation with Lansdale, Oppenheimer refused repeated attempts to get him to give out the name. "It is a question of some past loyalties," said Oppenheimer, who added that he would regard it as a "low trick" to disclose the name.

While they talked, Lansdale mentioned the names of several of Oppenheimer's acquaintances who were involved with leftist groups. "What about Haakon Chevalier?" Lansdale asked.

"Is he a member of the party?" Oppenheimer replied.

"I don't know," Lansdale said.

"He is a member of the faculty," Oppenheimer said, "and I know him well. I wouldn't be surprised if he were a member; he is quite a Red."

Finally, on December 12, 1943, during a visit to Los Alamos, General Groves ordered Oppenheimer to give him the name of the faculty member in question. At that point, Oppenheimer gave him the name of Haakon Chevalier.

There are few records of that conversation between Oppenheimer and Groves or of what Oppenheimer actually admitted about his contact with Chevalier concerning Eltenton. It's not known whether Oppenheimer gave Groves the names of any of the other physicists supposedly contacted by the "nameless intermediary."

The next day telegrams were sent to various security officers on the Manhattan Project identifying Chevalier as the professor who made contacts for Eltenton. Shortly after Groves and Oppenheimer had their conversation, Chevalier was called into the Office of War Information and told that he could not get the necessary clearance for a job in New York that he had been trying to get.

The whole incident raised many questions about Oppenheimer's character and life that were never to be answered. Were there three physicists involved in the contacts with Chevalier or had Oppenheimer made up that part of the story as he was to claim later?

If he did make up the story of the other contacts, why did he do so? Was he trying to draw suspicion from someone else, for example, his brother, who was so active in left-wing activities? Why did he wait so long to tell the security officers about the incident with Chevalier? And if it had been a purely innocent conversation between Oppenheimer and Chevalier, why did Oppenheimer create all of these complications for someone who was supposed to be a friend?

"Maintain the hope"

All the while Oppenheimer was battling security officials and worrying over how to answer their questions, he was also directing the Los Alamos scientists in trying to solve the problem of how to put together the bomb.

After the first conferences were held for physicists in the spring of 1943 at Los Alamos, Seth Neddermeyer, the California Institute of Technology physicist, began working on his proposals for an implosion assembly for the bomb. He had Oppenheimer's blessing to go ahead but no staff to help him.

Neddermeyer's crusade was a lonely one, and he got no encouragement from the man he reported to, Captain William "Deke" Parsons, who led the Ordnance Division at Los Alamos.

While Parsons and his crew pressed on with testing the gun method for both plutonium and uranium, Neddermeyer tested his implosion apparatus in a canyon just south of the laboratory. He would pack masses of TNT into a pipe surrounding another inner pipe and then detonate the little bomb. Then he would recover the blasted pipe to see if he had managed to create a symmetrical implosion, an explosion that would leave the pipe collapsed inward like a smashed beer can.

Although Oppenheimer let Neddermeyer continue his experiments, he did little to push them forward until a mathematician at Los Alamos calculated that implosion would produce more predictable results in a bomb than would the gun method. Edward Teller also suggested that the massive pressures produced in implosion would mean that less fissionable material could be used to touch off a chain reaction than would be needed with the gun method. Implosion could work in a bomb even if the plutonium used for the core was not completely pure.

Since extracting purified plutonium seemed as difficult at that point as sifting through a beach full of sand to find an ant, Neddermeyer's little explosions in the desert suddenly took on new meaning and purpose for Oppenheimer and other project leaders. If implosion could be perfected, it might mean that months could be saved in the drive for the bomb.

By the end of 1943 Oppenheimer and Groves were pouring dollars and staff hours into the implosion project. But soon clashing egos interfered with scientific progress. Tension grew between Neddermeyer and Parsons, partly stemming from Parsons's early lack of faith in the implosion method.

After learning of the new scientific conclusions about implosion, Parsons had committed himself to working harder on the method that he had once been cynical about. But the growing staff of scientists in the implosion group said he was too absorbed in details, too military-oriented due to his navy background. At the same time Parsons accused the scientists of being too "scientific," too ready to drop a technical problem as soon as they saw they could solve it, according to a letter Oppenheimer later wrote to Groves.

Oppenheimer said he was "in full sympathy" with Parsons but also said: "For the most part these men [scientists in the laboratory] regard their work here not as a scientific adventure, but as a responsible mission which will have failed if it is let drop at the laboratory phase."[1]

To introduce new drive and purpose to the project, Oppenheimer had to find a new leader, someone who could mold the warring factions into a fighting team. His choice was the energetic and hardworking George B. Kistiakowsky, a Russian-born chemist from Harvard who joined the staff in February 1944, at first as a consultant to Parsons. Although Kistiakowsky began to move the work ahead, he too had conflicts with Parsons and some with Neddermeyer.

Then a new discovery put more pressure on those working on implosion. The Italian physicist Emilio Segrè announced that his research on plutonium indicated that only the implosion method could produce a bomb made from plutonium. The gun method would work only with uranium 235.

It was clear that if the laboratory was going to make a bomb out of plutonium, which was most likely to be the first material that Hanford and Oak Ridge could supply to the laboratory, implosion had to be perfected, and fast. One difficulty for Kistiakowsky and the others was finding out what was happening when an implosion occurred. At first they could do no more than keep imploding their dummy bombs and analyzing the blasted metal casings left behind. Later they used electronic devices and cameras to detect what was going on. Some of the very early IBM computers also were brought in to help solve equations too difficult to calculate by hand.

Even so, the results of the implosion team were so crude that Oppenheimer decided that whatever device was developed would require a full-scale bomb test before the weapon could actually be used.

A breakthrough came in early 1944 when some British scientists visited the laboratory and proposed a new way of touching off a symmetrical explosion for the implosion bomb. Their idea was to surround the central core with layers of slow and fast explosives that would produce a powerful and symmetrical shock wave directed toward the central core of plutonium. They called this arrangement of explosives a "lens" because it reflected shock waves in a way similar to that of optical lenses in reflecting light.

The concept seemed like the answer, but it required a dramatic change in direction for those working on implosion. After one experiment on the device, which had been nicknamed "the gadget," Kistiakowsky wrote in his diary: "The test of the gadget failed. Project staff resumes frantic work. Kistiakowsky goes nuts and is locked up!"[2]

As tension and pressure grew, it became clear to Oppenheimer that he had to reorganize the laboratory. To begin with, he needed more and more skilled technicians and junior scientists. Increasingly, the laboratory was competing with the military services that were drafting key people to help fight the war. The army was persuaded to help and created the Special Engineer Detachment, which channeled hundreds of enlisted men and women into Los Alamos.

At that point Oppenheimer decided to put Kistiakowsky and Robert F. Bacher in place of Neddermeyer to head the work on implosion. These men drew their staff from those under Parsons, who was now working on getting a bomber ready to carry the weapon. Neddermeyer became a group leader under Bacher.

Again and again, Oppenheimer was to do this during the last year at Los Alamos. He would organize new groups to take over tasks and appoint new leaders in an effort to keep the project moving on time. In the early months at Los Alamos, Oppenheimer had managed to hold back the sharp and biting sarcasm that wounded friends and created enemies. But now, due to fatigue and stress, he had lost some of this control.

Neddermeyer felt betrayed by the way Oppenheimer had handled his case. "A lot of people looked up to him as a source of wisdom and inspiration," he later said. "I respected him as a scientist, but I just didn't look up to him that way. . . . From my point of view, he was an intellectual snob. He could cut you cold and humiliate you right down to the ground."[3]

Another headache for Oppenheimer was the struggle to get the necessary materials and equipment needed for the laboratory. Because purchasing had to be done under cover of complete secrecy, materials were ordered from offices in Los Angeles or Chicago and then shipped on to Los Alamos. But this meant that the Los Alamos staff couldn't talk directly to suppliers; shipments were often delayed or arrived carrying the wrong materials or equipment. Oppenheimer struggled to get the University of California to help and to get the chief purchasing agent to visit the laboratory.

In April 1945 the shattering news hit Los Alamos that President Franklin Roosevelt had died. The feeling was that the nation had lost a great leader, that suddenly the country had no one to lead it to an end to the war that still raged on in the Pacific.

On a snowy Sunday at the Los Alamos movie theater that served as the site for church services, Oppenheimer spoke of the loss and comforted the little laboratory community. "One is reminded of medieval days, when the death of a good and wise and just king plunged his country into despair, and mourning," Oppenheimer said.

"The faith of Roosevelt is one that is shared by millions of men and women in every country of the world. For this reason it is possible to maintain the hope, for this reason it is right that we should dedicate ourselves to the hope, that his good works will not have ended with his death."[4]

Although such moments made the group feel like a family, the reality was that staff members frequently clashed with each other, both in the laboratory and after work. The barracks-like homes, crude as they were, were snapped up like mansions by millionaires. Scientists had the first crack at them, which rankled the technicians who because of the housing crisis were offered bonuses to leave their families at home.

Oppenheimer was insulated from this struggle. He lived in a comfortable bungalow on what was nicknamed Bathtub Row, a street of houses that had once been buildings at the Ranch School and most of which had bathtubs. Many homes thrown up at Los Alamos during the war had only showers.

Soon after the Oppenheimers arrived at Los Alamos, Kitty Oppenheimer gave birth to their second child, a baby girl, Toni. Kitty found bringing up a baby at Los Alamos was something like taking a baby on a backpacking trip, what with shortages of supplies like baby bottles.

Mrs. Oppenheimer didn't seem to adjust well to life on the mesa even though she made a stab at putting her biology background to work in the laboratory. She had always been a heavy drinker, and she continued at parties at Los Alamos. She kept largely in the background of Oppenheimer's life in New Mexico and sometimes even took shopping trips to the West Coast, leaving her children behind with a maid.

But she and Oppenheimer remained close. In spite of his heavy work schedule they often rode in the mountains on horses they kept in the Ranch School stables. Sometimes they also slipped away for dinner alone or with friends at a nearby tearoom run by Edith Warner, an older woman who had moved to New Mexico in the 1920s for her health. Oppenheimer made a special arrangement for Miss Warner to serve dinner two or three times a week to groups of scientists and their wives from Los Alamos. He had seen the need for workers unable to leave New Mexico for any length of time to have a getaway spot.

By the end of 1944 there had been some encouraging breakthroughs on the bomb assembly. The group working on the gun design that would use uranium 235 had completed a number of favorable tests and was ready to freeze in place a design for this bomb. Since Oppenheimer was sure the gun would work and was also sure that he wouldn't have spare uranium on hand to make a test bomb, it was decided to assemble the gun without any prior testing.

Implosion was a different story. Although testing on the implosion design had improved, Oppenheimer still felt that a full-scale test was needed before the implosion bomb could be used on a real target. But what if the test should be a dud, and all of the precious plutonium used in the bomb were lost?

Just in case, the scientists at Los Alamos decided to design and contract for Jumbo, a 214-ton steel tank. The idea was that the plutonium bomb would be blasted off inside the tank, allowing the fragments of plutonium to be recovered.

9

"Break, blow, burn and make me new"

As the summer of 1945 wore on and the day of the plutonium bomb test drew near, dry desert winds scorched Los Alamos. The grass withered, and needles on the pine trees turned to tinder. At times the sky would grow heavy with gloomy purple clouds, and lightning crackled over distant mountains, but no rain fell. Water supplies were cherished drop by drop for fear that a forest fire might break out nearby and ignite the makeshift settlement of wooden buildings. The sultry weather and water shortages combined to make tempers grow short among Los Alamos scientists as they raced to meet a deadline for the atom bomb test.

The strain of running Los Alamos had halted the occasional horseback riding trips that Robert Oppenheimer loved to take in the nearby canyons and hills with his wife, Kitty. In addition, he had fallen ill with chicken pox, which had struck many children in the Los Alamos complex. His suits and the blue jeans and checked shirts he wore occasionally hung limply on his six-foot-tall frame as his weight dropped thirty pounds to one hundred fifteen.

Pressed by the army to test the bomb by mid-July, Oppenheimer began to look drawn and preoccupied. When fellow workers said good morning to him, he hardly seemed to notice, and he rarely answered. His nerves grew tenser, and a lack of sleep sapped his energy.

In May 1945 the Germans surrendered, and security forces quickly determined that Germany had not produced an atom bomb. But the fact that it was no longer necessary to drop an atom bomb on Germany seemed to make little difference in the work schedule on the mesa at Los Alamos. Japan fought fiercely despite the fact that its navy was nearly destroyed and B-29 bombing raids had shattered many of its cities. American leaders believed Japan might not surrender until the Allies invaded the country, and they predicted that such a landing in Japan might cost a half-million lives. More and more, the use of the atomic bomb was considered as a way to avoid that prospect provided that it could be developed in time. "In such a climate," said General Leslie Groves, "no one who held a position of responsibility in the Manhattan Project could doubt that we were trying to perfect a weapon that, however repugnant it might be to us as human beings, could nonetheless save untold numbers of American lives."[1]

In early May a Target Committee, on which Oppenheimer served as an adviser, met at Los Alamos and discussed at what height the bomb should be detonated, what its effects might be, whether to hold possible rehearsals of a bombing, and what Japanese cities might become bomb targets.

Among the cities the committee proposed for study were Kyoto, Hiroshima, Niigata, and Kokura Arsenal. The final choice of a target was made by President Truman in consultation with Secretary of War Henry Stimson. In the end, Hiroshima was chosen, partly because it had so far escaped major damage in the war, partly because it was a strategic port, and partly because the Japanese army headquarters was located there. Also, Stimson objected strongly to bombing Kyoto, which was a Buddhist and Shinto religious center thronged with shrines and temples.

At about the same time Truman and Stimson had set up a group of officials and politicians, called the Interim Committee, to advise the president on whether the bomb should be used at all and how it should be controlled in future. The committee received advice from a Scientific Panel made up of Oppenheimer, Enrico Fermi, Arthur Compton, and Ernest Lawrence. On May 31 the Interim Committee and the Scientific Panel met to discuss how atomic weapons should be controlled after the war. Oppenheimer urged that the United States offer the world free information on atomic bombs, with particular emphasis on peacetime uses.

Ernest Lawrence, also at the meeting, had a different viewpoint. If the United States was to stay ahead in atomic energy, he declared, it must know more than any other power. That meant strenuous research must continue. Oppenheimer disagreed. He felt that the scientists tied to atomic research should go back to their previous jobs and proceed in research at a more leisurely pace.

Later that day the group turned to a more immediate question: Should the atomic bomb be dropped on Japan at all? Ernest Lawrence suggested that the new weapon should be used in some kind of demonstration for Japan rather than actually being exploded on some city.

But Oppenheimer said he could not think of a demonstration spectacular enough to convince the Japanese that the United States had a totally new and different weapon. What if the bomb was a dud or if the Japanese sabotaged the test in some way? Possibly the Japanese would try to shoot down the plane flying the bomb to the demonstration site?

"You ask yourself would the Japanese government as then

constituted and with divisions between the peace party and the war party, would it have been influenced by an enormous nuclear firecracker detonated at a great height doing little damage and your answer is as good as mine. I don't know," Oppenheimer later reflected.[2]

In the end the Interim Committee and its scientific advisers recommended using the bomb on Japan without any prior warning. The most desirable target, the group decided, would be a war plant or military installation of some kind employing a large number of workers and closely surrounded by workers' houses.

Many people have asked why Oppenheimer or someone else on the committee did not raise any strong objections to this recommendation, particularly since Oppenheimer already knew about the doubts of many scientists concerning use of the bomb. Many had joined the battle to build the bomb because they were refugees, driven out of Europe by Hitler. Now that the bomb was not needed against Germany, they questioned whether it should be used at all. And if it were used on Japan with no warning to either Japan or the rest of the world, what would be the chances of persuading other nations to join in international control of peacetime uses of the atom?

"I set forth my anxieties and the arguments . . . against dropping [the bomb] . . . but I did not endorse them," Oppenheimer said later about his role with the Interim Committee and the Scientific Panel.[3]

Did he think that the advice of scientists wouldn't be taken seriously by those in political power? Or was he too close to the immediate technical problem of building the bomb to think about the long-range effects of its use?

Of course, Oppenheimer did not have the final say on what would happen to Japan. Many other officials were involved. "It was up to the president as to what to do with it," said physicist I. I. Rabi. "People forget we had a president when they ask questions."[4]

At the time the committee was meeting to decide about the bomb, another group of scientists, including the renowned Niels Bohr and James Franck, pleaded with President Truman and other officials not to drop the bomb until Japan was fully warned of what was to happen and still refused to surrender. They put together what was known as the Franck Report, proposing that instead of bombing Japan the United States should demonstrate the new weapon before representatives of a number of nations, in a desert or on a barren island. They warned: "The military advantages and the saving of American lives achieved by the sudden use of atomic bombs against Japan may be outweighed by the ensuing loss of confidence and by a wave of horror and repulsion sweeping over the rest of the world. . . ."[5]

A leader of the group was Leo Szilard, the refugee physicist who had once tried to persuade the president to press ahead with atomic research. Szilard contacted Edward Teller and urged him to circulate a petition at Los Alamos that would be sent to Truman. The petition argued that exploding the bomb in Japan would open "the door to an era of devastation on an unimaginable scale."[6]

Teller claimed that he went to see Oppenheimer about the petition and was given a fairly cold reception. "He assured me that the right decisions would be made by the leaders in Washington who were wise people and understood the psychology of the Japanese," Teller said.[7]

Because of this incident, Teller said he backed out of the petition effort and wrote to Szilard: "The things we are working on are so terrible that no amount of protesting or fiddling with politics will save our souls."[8]

In later life Oppenheimer regretted that he had not taken a stronger stand against direct use of the bomb on Japan, but he never said that the United States should not have developed the bomb, nor did he regret his role at Los Alamos.

In a speech to the scientists at Los Alamos just before he

left, Oppenheimer said: "When you come right down to it the reason we did this job is because it was an organic necessity. If you are a scientist you cannot stop such a thing. If you are a scientist you believe that it is good to find out how the world works; that it is good to find out what the realities are; that it is good to turn over to mankind at large the greatest possible power to control the world and to deal with it according to its lights and its values."[9]

At the beginning of July, Robert Oppenheimer was asked to move the bomb test up by six days, to July 14, so that President Truman could present the evidence of the test at a meeting he was holding with Joseph Stalin of the U.S.S.R. in Potsdam, Germany. Truman believed that with the bomb as part of the country's arsenal he would have a stronger diplomatic position in talks with Stalin about the future of Eastern Europe and Germany.

But as the clock kept ticking, the project ran into problems with the molds being used to make the lenses for the bomb. The lenses were the devices that would ensure that an explosion inside the bomb would take place evenly around the radioactive core. As the implosion group worked to repair the lens molds, Oppenheimer decided that the test could not be moved ahead. The earliest possible date would be July 16.

Throughout the spring Oppenheimer and Kenneth Bainbridge, who was put in charge of the test, had roamed the western United States to find a site that was fairly close to Los Alamos but also well isolated.

They looked at a desert area near Rice, California, a portion of the Mojave Desert in California, the sand dunes of Colorado's San Luis Valley, and several other spots.

Finally they agreed on a site two hundred miles from Los Alamos in an area of southern New Mexico that the early Spanish conquistadores had called Jornada del Muerto, or the Journey of Death. It was a place of burning alkali sands spotted with yucca, sagebrush, and Joshua trees that was home to gila monsters and scorpions. Fierce winds and thunderstorms sometimes swept this patch of desert, but for the most part it was drought-stricken, baked by temperatures that often rose above one hundred degrees.

Some three hundred workers prepared at this site for the arrival of the plutonium-fueled implosion bomb that was to be detonated at a spot dubbed Point Zero. There contractors built a 110-foot-high lattice structure that looked something like an oil derrick. At the top the bomb (nicknamed Fat Man) would be enclosed in a small hutlike structure. The scientists at Los Alamos had decided to hang the bomb on a tower in order to minimize possible fallout of nuclear waste in a dust cloud. They no longer planned to use Jumbo, the giant tank. The fact was they didn't know exactly how much fallout there would be or where it would go. Strong winds or unusual weather could easily spread nuclear waste into towns and cities hundreds of miles away.

At various points some ten thousand yards away from the Point Zero tower workers built observation bunkers. The one at the south point, code-named Baker, was where Oppenheimer and the other officials and scientists would watch the test. It had its own telephone and was connected by radio to scientists and military personnel out in the field.

When the metal tower at Point Zero was complete, B-29s began making test runs over it. When the test actually took place, a crew was supposed to buzz close to the tower just before detonation, drop an instrument package in place of the real bomb, and then speed away, in a dress rehearsal of what would happen over Japan.

Although the test was an official secret, many people not actually involved in building the bomb knew that something momentous was about to happen, including wives and children of some of the scientists.

The code word "Trinity" was used to talk about it. Use of this name puzzled many people. Why refer to the testing of something that would unleash terrible forces of death and destruction on the world with a word that was associated with churches and Christianity and God?

After the war General Groves asked Oppenheimer why he had chosen the name, and Oppenheimer wrote back: "Why I chose the name is not clear, but I know what thoughts were in my mind. There is a poem of John Donne, written just before his death, which I know and love. . . ."[10]

In that poem Donne, a seventeenth-century English clergyman, writes about the Trinity of God:

Batter my heart, three-personed God, for you
As yet but knock, breathe, shine and seek to mend.
That I may rise and stand, o'erthrow me and bend
Your force to break, blow, burn, and make me new.

By that point the scientists at Los Alamos had begun to indulge in a form of gallows humor—bets as to how big the size of the atom bomb test burst would be. They measured its size by comparing it to the bang produced by various amounts of TNT. Physicist Edward Teller, who would later develop the hydrogen bomb, made the biggest estimate—forty-five thousand tons of TNT. Someone even bet on zero. Oppenheimer, perhaps as a result of the strain he was working under, bet on a very low figure—three hundred tons.

Finally, problems with the lens molds were solved, and on July 5 Oppenheimer sent the following telegram to physicists Ernest Lawrence at the University of California at Berkeley and Arthur Compton at the University of Chicago to let them know the test would be held soon and they should come out to Los Alamos:

ANY TIME AFTER THE 15TH WOULD BE A GOOD TIME FOR OUR FISHING TRIP. BECAUSE WE ARE NOT CERTAIN OF THE WEATHER WE MAY BE DELAYED SEVERAL DAYS. WE DO NOT

A series of dress rehearsals was held for the big Trinity test. First a mock-up plutonium assembly was driven over the Los Alamos mesa to see how it could take the bumps. The mock-up was driven to the site, unloaded, assembled on the tower, and then returned to Los Alamos. The whole process was repeated a second time.

On Wednesday, July 11, the exodus of scientists began from Los Alamos as they headed for Trinity with the equipment for the bomb test. That afternoon Robert Oppenheimer went through stacks of papers in his office and gave final instructions to his secretary. She noticed that he seemed distracted, and she was sure that something important was about to happen. At about 7 P.M. he walked home to say good-bye to his wife, Kitty, and his children, baby daughter Toni and Peter, three, before driving to Trinity. Kitty gave him a good-luck charm, a four-leaf clover she had found in their backyard. They had worked out a code message for him to send to her if the test was a success: "You can change the sheets."

The next day at 3 P.M., Philip Morrison, who had once been a student in Oppenheimer's physics classes, removed the plutonium core of the bomb from a nuclear-materials vault in Los Alamos Canyon. The core was made up of several ingots of plutonium, which were packed into two special valises for the journey to Trinity. The valises were connected to thermometers to measure the plutonium's radioactivity, and each valise was protected against corrosion, against dropping into water, and against overheating. But Morrison was worried about the possibility of an automobile accident on the way to the site that might set off an explosion. So an escort car filled with security men led the way, and behind them rode another car filled with members of the nuclear assembly team.

Five hours later the little procession turned off a dirt road and stopped at an abandoned adobe ranchhouse near the Trinity site. One room of the ranchhouse had been fitted out as an assembly room for the bomb core. The room had been carefully vacuumed and its windows sealed against dust with black masking tape. After depositing the valises on a table in the room, Morrison went to bed.

While he slept, back at Los Alamos the second major part of the bomb, the explosive assembly, was being packed into a truck for transport to Trinity. Chemist George Kistiakowsky, head of the implosion group, put the explosive assembly, nicknamed "the gadget," into a special metal container covered with a waterproof casing. The whole contraption was packaged in a wooden crate and put onto an Army truck, where it was lashed onto a special steel bed and covered with a tarpaulin.

Kistiakowsky and the explosive assembly set off for Trinity accompanied by three jeeps full of military police and two sedans with security agents. The trip was supposed to be a secret, quiet affair, but every time they rode through a town, the security police would switch on sirens and red lights. The idea was to scare off drunken drivers, but the noise woke up sleeping residents along the way.

When the entourage arrived, its members found the Trinity base camp in an uproar. Oppenheimer had been up most of the night because of the failure of one of the preliminary tests for the bomb. The scientists had been trying out the bomb's firing circuits by using a chunk of high explosive to simulate the bomb. No explosion occurred, not even a puff of smoke. "Oppie—he was very nervy—came down like a ton of bricks on me," Kistiakowsky later said. Kistiakowsky and another scientist took the unit apart and discovered that it had been tested so much that it had overheated and some of the solder joints had melted. "After all, the thing had been designed only to be used once sitting on the bomb, and it must have been tested hundreds of times. So, anyway, that minor storm passed," Kistiakowsky said.[12]

The next morning at nine the final assembly of the bomb began. In the ranchhouse assembly room eight scientists in white surgical coats hovered around a table where the plutonium ingots lay on wrapping paper. As Geiger counters clicked and MPs stood guard outside, Canadian scientist Louis Slotin pushed the plutonium pieces together to the point where they were almost critical, or almost unstable enough to start a nuclear chain reaction. One slip and the entire group might be exposed to radiation that would cause a slow, painful death. In fact, four jeeps stood parked outside the house with their motors running, waiting for a quick getaway in case Slotin accidentally started a chain reaction.

Every few minutes Oppenheimer stopped by to visit. There was nothing he could do to help, but he wanted to watch the tense little operation. But after a while his nervousness and pacing began to bother the men, and they asked politely that he leave.

The final step was for Slotin to wedge between the pieces of plutonium what was known as an "initiator," a tiny cylinder that would send out a neutron pulse to start the chain reaction at the core of the bomb.

At the same time Kistiakowsky and his team spent the day preparing the explosive assembly for the insertion of the core. Finally, both crews had finished their individual jobs and it was time to put the two pieces together. The eighty-pound core, or plug, was laid on a litter and carried out of the ranchhouse to a car that drove to the tower at Point Zero.

Inside a tent under the tower the core was put onto a manually operated hoist and raised above Kistiakowsky's explosive assembly before being slowly lowered into it. Again the Geiger counters ticked ominously; the subcritical parts of the core were held apart by so little that a knock could start a chain reaction.

Suddenly the plug stuck, and apprehension froze every

one in the tent, including Oppenheimer. In previous tests with dummies, the apparatus had always fit together smoothly. Then one of the scientists, Robert Bacher, determined that the plug had expanded because it was producing heat. The crew decided to leave the pieces next to each other for a while in hopes that they would reach a temperature equilibrium. Moments later the insertion was tried again, and the core slipped in smoothly. At 10 P.M. the bomb assembly was complete.

But then there were new anxieties. After months of heat the drought had broken, and a number of storms had been forecast. A team of weathermen who floated weather balloons up over the site every few hours predicted the storms might last for at least two days. That would mean that rain might create dangerous fallout of radioactive material in the local area instead of winds blowing and scattering the material into the upper atmosphere. Oppenheimer wondered if the test should be put off until the weather improved.

The same morning Oppenheimer received a call from Los Alamos saying that a test on a dummy explosive assembly, similar to the one on the tower at Point Zero, had failed. The assembly had not produced the symmetrical shock waves needed to create the biggest explosion possible but instead had produced an explosion that was completely disorganized. The team members at Los Alamos told Oppenheimer they thought the bomb would fail.

After the weeks of tension and previous setbacks, Oppenheimer lashed out in anger again at Kistiakowsky.

"I was accused this time of failing the project, of being the cause of embarrassment to everybody from Oppie upwards," Kistiakowsky said.

Oppenheimer paced, nervous and upset, and Kistiakowsky offered him a bet: one month's salary against ten dollars that the bomb would work. Oppenheimer took the bet, and Kistiakowsky walked off angrily.[13]

10

"I am become Death"

Oppenheimer got little sleep on Saturday night. Part of the time he spent with Donald Hornig trying to figure out why the firing circuits had failed. For another four hours he tossed restlessly on his bed in a cubicle in a hut at the base camp. Someone who slept nearby heard him coughing constantly as he ran over the options in his mind. Should the test be canceled? What was the sense in continuing? If the test was scratched, could they ever try again?

In the midst of these worries he searched for some emotional comfort from the *Bhagavad-Gita*, the Indian poem he had studied at Harvard in the original Sanskrit. Many Western thinkers have been influenced by the *Gita*, an eighteen-part dialogue between a warrior prince and Krishna, the Indian god. To Oppenheimer the epic poem had become something of a bible, particularly during his years at Los Alamos.

That night he quoted from the poem to Vannevar Bush, the Manhattan District official who had come to Alamogordo for the test: "In sleep, in confusion, in the depths of shame, the good deeds a man has done before defend him."[1]

Sunday morning brought relief. As Oppenheimer sipped his breakfast coffee, he received a call from Hans Bethe in Los Alamos. The results of the implosion experiment were meaningless, Bethe told him. Even a perfect implosion wouldn't have produced oscilloscope records any different from those the tests created. Bethe couldn't assure Oppenheimer that the test had been a success, but he couldn't say it had been a failure either.

Hornig had better news for Oppenheimer. The blown detonator circuits had worn out because scientists had overworked the dummy firing unit through endless experiments. The new circuits on the bomb on top of the tower should work just fine.

The next worry was the weather. Although the sun seared the men who were adjusting cameras in the desert and placing instruments around the shot tower, the predictions were for rains and wind to come. Among those setting up equipment was Robert Oppenheimer's brother, Frank, who placed boxes filled with bits of paper and posts nailed with iron strips in the Ground Zero area. He was trying to simulate in crude form the paper-style houses that a bomb might hit in Japan.

By midafternoon thunder rumbled over the desert, and weathermen sent up balloons, trying to interpret the winds and clouds. But the forecast seemed all right—the skies should clear by dawn, and it was unlikely that the radioactive cloud from the test would drift into a thunderhead and scatter fallout on people and houses. All that afternoon scientists and high-ranking military officers arrived at Alamogordo. As evening came, other workers who had been left behind at Los Alamos also packed up to go to the test site.

At 4 P.M. Sunday, Oppenheimer and Groves met with the weathermen for a conference at the ranch house that was a short distance from Ground Zero, the place where the bomb would explode. Chief weatherman Jack Hubbard told the two, who kept nervously checking the skies outside, that the shot could go ahead as scheduled but weather conditions weren't perfect. Oppenheimer and Groves discussed the situation and agreed to have a final weather conference Monday morning at two, when they would decide if the test could go off as planned at four.

Early in the evening Oppenheimer climbed the hundred-foot steel tower to view the final product of the two years of struggle at Los Alamos. There the five-foot sphere of high explosives and plutonium sat on an oak platform sheltered by walls and a roof of corrugated iron. Embracing the gadget were long insulated wires that ended in suckerlike detonators clapped onto the sides of the bomb. The ugly, dark machine looked something like the head of Medusa, the gruesome monster of Greek mythology with hair like snakes. As the wind and thunder shook the tower, Oppenheimer checked the sixty-four detonators attached to the X-unit that would set off the blasts inside the explosives beneath the surface of the bomb.

The wild desert scene, lashed by the threat of storms, added drama to an already suspenseful moment. In a few hours the culmination of the Manhattan Project's $2 billion effort could change the world forever. Then again, the test could fizzle, leaving frustrated scientists who were trying to unlock the power of the atom.

Later Oppenheimer stood with an associate and watched the clouds blow up over the Sierra Oscura. "Funny how the mountains always inspire our work," he said.

Nearby, Enrico Fermi and some of his colleagues were trying to relieve pent-up tension by making bets on whether the bomb would ignite the atmosphere. If it did, would it just destroy New Mexico or the entire world? Even if the test bomb was a dud, Fermi joked, the experiment would have been worthwhile.

Groves was annoyed at the joking, and Alamogordo director Kenneth Bainbridge was furious when rumors of Fermi's comments spread through the camp. It made Oppenheimer realize more clearly what would happen if weather delayed the test. It would be a terrible blow to the overworked scientists who had been strained to the breaking point.

Pressure was building in the outside world as well. In Berlin President Truman and Winston Churchill had arrived to meet with Russia's dictator Joseph Stalin for the Potsdam conference. It was essential to Truman that the test go off as planned so that he would have a stronger negotiating position with Russia.

By midnight mist began to fall, and two hours later heavy rain drove across the desert while lightning lit up the sky. After consulting with weather forecasters again, Oppenheimer and Groves decided to delay the test shot until 5:30 A.M., but Oppenheimer kept telling Groves: "If we postpone, I'll never get my people up to pitch again."[2]

In spite of the storms General Groves insisted that a group of scientists camp out under the tower at Point Zero in case saboteurs should try to disturb the test.

Oppenheimer's nervousness increased when Enrico Fermi came to him and urged that the test be postponed because of the rain. He feared that the storm could deluge the test site with dangerous fallout. At that point Groves and Oppenheimer drove to the bunker at S. 10,000, the main control point for the Trinity test. This spot, ten thousand yards south of Ground Zero, was where Oppenheimer would observe the explosion.

At 4 A.M. the rain began to behave as the forecasters had predicted and started to move on. Bainbridge, Groves, and Oppenheimer concluded that the test could indeed take place at 5:30, just before dawn.

Kenneth Bainbridge sprang to action and drove to the

tower to begin the final preparations. There he threw an arming switch that would allow the bomb to be detonated from the bunker at S. 10,000. He and the other scientists who had been guarding the tower then returned to the control bunker.

Meanwhile, scientists and officials took positions around the test site. Busloads of Los Alamos staff members and others drove up to Compagna Hill, twenty miles northwest of Ground Zero. Among them were Edward Teller, Ernest Lawrence, and Hans Bethe. These observers were told to lie in the sand and bury their heads in their arms, but no one was ready to do that. Their scientific instincts got the better of them. They wanted to see what was going on. "We were determined to look the beast in the eye," Teller said.[3]

Some of the physicists and officials did apply the suntan lotion that Teller had brought, and others were ready to put on the welders' glasses that they had been ordered to wear.

General Groves, who had insisted for safety's sake that he and Oppenheimer view the test at different locations, drove back to the base camp to observe the test. Shallow trenches had been bulldozed there so that the observers at the base camp could lie down in them, since they were ten miles closer to Point Zero than the group at Compagna Hill.

At 5:10 A.M. Sam Allison, the staff member chosen to broadcast from the control center over loudspeakers spread across the desert, began the countdown: "It is now zero minus twenty minutes."

At the control center at S. 10,000, where Oppenheimer was watching the test, several workers jammed a twenty-foot-square room filled with controls and apparatus. No one would actually push a button to set off the gadget. An automatic timer that would be turned on in the last minute before the test would actually touch off the bomb. Donald Hornig monitored a switch that could cut the connection between the X-unit in the tower and the bomb if for some reason the test had to be interrupted at the last minute. As the countdown continued, rockets shot up at various points, and a siren at the base camp wailed in warning.

Oppenheimer stood in the control room doorway, where he kept an eye on the sky and weather but also watched over the workers in the shelter. To those around him he seemed torn between fear that the bomb would fail and fear that the world-shattering weapon would actually work. He turned to an officer next to him and said, "Lord, these affairs are hard on the heart."[4]

As the moments ticked off, Oppenheimer scarcely breathed, and he held onto a post to steady himself. At forty-five seconds before zero a worker flipped the switch for the automatic timer, and the device began triggering circuits one after another.

Sam Allison boomed out: "Zero minus ten seconds!" and then "Zero minus three seconds!" In the last instant a quirky fear seized Allison. Would the explosion act like lightning and electrocute him through the microphone he gripped? At minus one second he dropped the microphone and yelled, "Zero!"[5]

In that instant voltage shot through the firing unit to touch off the bomb.

At 5:29:45 A.M. Mountain War Time, July 16, 1945, a great green super-sun rose above the desert. In less than a second it had climbed to more than eight thousand feet. Its light filled the sky with dazzling intensity.

Bill Laurence, a *New York Times* reporter who was allowed to observe the test later wrote: "Up it went, a great ball of fire about a mile in diameter, changing colors as it kept shooting upward, from deep purple to orange, expanding, growing bigger, rising as it expanded, an elemental force freed from its bonds after being chained for billions of years. For a fleeting instant, the color was unearthly green, such as one sees only in the corona of the sun during a total eclipse. It was as though the earth had opened and the skies had split."[6]

All who saw it described the light as the brightest they had ever seen. In a single instant searing sunshine shot across the darkened desert, turning night to day. It seemed to many observers that the bomb cloud hung above them in almost total silence. Then a dust cloud grew out of the skirt of the mighty fireball overhead, and the ball rose again and formed a giant mushroom.

Splitting the silence, thunder echoed back and forth against the mountains fringing the Alamogordo desert. The ground trembled and a wave of hot wind touched the faces of those watching the test. As the boom hit the trench that Groves was lying in, he muttered, "We must keep this whole thing quiet."

"I think they heard the noise in five states," an army associate said in reply.[7]

"A few people laughed, a few people cried, most people were silent," Oppenheimer said later. "There floated through my mind a line from the Bhagavad-Gita in which Krishna is trying to persuade the prince that he should do his duty: 'I am become death, the shatterer of worlds.' "[8]

Like Oppenheimer, others viewed the blast as if it were something of a religious experience. One army official wrote that the blast "made us feel we puny things were blasphemous to dare tamper with the forces heretofore reserved for the Almighty."[9]

Many watchers were flooded with the ecstasy of success as they slapped each other on the back and shook hands. At the base camp paper cups of whisky were passed around in celebration.

Kistiakowsky had been watching from the top of the control bunker at S.10,000. He ran up and threw his arms around Oppenheimer. "Oppie, Oppie," he cried, "I won the bet. You owe me ten dollars."

Still shaken by the bomb's power, Oppenheimer opened

his wallet and replied seriously, "It's empty, you'll have to wait." The two men embraced.[10]

Kenneth Bainbridge shook Oppenheimer's hand and said, "Oppie, now we're all sons of bitches."[11]

As Oppenheimer drove back to base camp, he was filled with new confidence. The achievement had overwhelmed all who had watched the test. As soon as he arrived, he had his secretary phone his wife. "Tell her she can change the sheets," he said.[12]

He also telegraphed his Chicago colleague Arthur Compton: "You'll be interested to know we caught a very big fish."[13]

Groves sent a message to Potsdam: "Doctor has just returned most enthusiastic and confident that the little boy is as husky as his big brother. The light in his eyes discernible from here to Highhold and I could hear his screams from here to my farm."[14]

Groves's message was clear: he was sure the uranium gun bomb ("little boy"), already set out on its journey to Japan, would be as potent as the plutonium bomb ("big brother").

Eight days later President Truman told Stalin that the United States had a potent weapon, and Stalin seemed to be strangely unsurprised. What Truman didn't know at the time was that spies from the Los Alamos test site had already passed on information about the atomic bomb. At that point the Russians might have been building a bomb of their own.

Within a few hours, however, foreboding over what was to come next, over what the bomb meant to the world, began to replace the euphoria at the test site. Already Groves had announced to a colleague, "The war is over as soon as we drop two of these on Japan."[15]

One scientist was later horrified to hear a Washington official at the base camp explain why it would be better to cremate Japanese civilians with the new weapon than to lose a million American lives by attempting an invasion of Japan.

Within moments after the test a group of three scientists, including Enrico Fermi, had donned white surgical costumes and driven in tanks out into the desert to Ground Zero. They planned to take soil samples from a trap door in the bottom of the tank.

As they rumbled up to the site, their Geiger counters clicked wildly. At the spot where the tower had once stood holding the bomb, nothing remained except for jagged stumps of twisted metal.

Surrounding the tower was what looked like a twelve-hundred-foot saucer of green glass. The bomb had sucked up the desert sands, melted them with its terrifying heat, and dumped the molten mass back on the test site. The emerald-colored beads surrounding the tower would be christened "pearls of Trinity," or trinitite.

Nothing remained alive in the area—no rattlesnake or lizard or insect. The yuccas and Joshua trees had disappeared. The bits of paper and metal that Frank Oppenheimer had tacked up at the site had evaporated.

The Jumbo tank, which in the end was not used to enclose the bomb but had been hung from a tower near the test site, was lying unscathed on the ground, but its tower too had been blasted to pieces.

No one doubted the terrible power of the gadget. Its force was estimated as being equal to more than eighteen thousand tons of TNT.

For Oppenheimer, however, the chill of what the bomb might do to Japan had not yet settled on him. At Los Alamos that night a party was held at Oppenheimer's home that lasted far into the night. Later he would return to Ground Zero himself to view the test tower. A series of photographs was taken on the occasion: Oppenheimer with Groves and Oppenheimer with a group of scientists. In these photographs Oppenheimer still looks wan and wasted from his ordeal, but everyone is smiling and relaxed. As Oppenheimer reviews the results of radioactive tests on samples of sand, he looks as if he is reviewing production records for some factory or attending a ground-breaking for a housing project. Little about the photo indicates the fear and confusion that had begun to fall over the scientists at Los Alamos.

As a young man, Oppenheimer was camera shy. This is said to be the first public newsphoto, taken in 1935 at Cal Tech. Left to right: *Dr. P. A. M. Dirac, Robert A. Millikan—both Nobel Prize-winning scientists, and Oppenheimer.*

*Oppenheimer and Major General
Leslie R. Groves inspect the melted
remains of the steel tower
on which the first atomic
bomb was positioned.*

*A study of Oppenheimer as he appeared
in New York City in 1945 to attend
conferences that would deal with the
development of atomic energy use.*

In 1946, Oppenheimer and group of distinguished scientists examined the vacuum chamber of the University of California's 184-inch cyclotron. This was the first photo of the cyclotron released to the public.

Left: *Another photo, taken at about the same time, of Professor Ernest O. Lawrence and Oppenheimer in the accelerating chamber of the cyclotron.* Above: *Oppenheimer and the bomb seen here with Henry DeWolf Smyth, Glenn Seaborg, and Kenneth D. Nichols.*

Oppenheimer and Brien McMahon are shown after Oppenheimer testified before the Joint Congressional Atomic Energy Commission in 1949.

*Oppenheimer posed for this portrait at Princeton's
Institute for Advanced Study in 1954 shortly
after he had been suspended from his position as
consultant to the Atomic Energy Commission.*

A rare photograph of the private man, Oppenheimer is shown here arriving in Paris in 1958 with his wife and daughter.

*In the same year, Oppenheimer went to Israel for
the opening of the Israeli Institute of Nuclear Science.
He is shown here seated between Prime Minister
David Ben-Gurion and Ben-Gurion's wife Paula.*

*At the White House in late 1963,
Lyndon B. Johnson presented the
Enrico Fermi award—one of science's
most coveted honors—to Oppenheimer.
Ironically, the signature on the
certificate was that of John F. Kennedy,
whose assassination had
occurred only the previous week.*

In 1966, a frail Oppenheimer (at far left) *was given an honorary degree at Princeton. At his side* (from left to right) *are astronaut Charles Conrad; Princeton's president at the time, Robert F. Goheen; Secretary of Health, Education and Welfare John W. Gardner; and Attorney General Nicholas D. Katzenbach.*

11

"The reaction has begun"

After that it seemed as if machinery was set in motion that no one could stop.

Soon after the test several scientists from Los Alamos flew to Tinian, an island in the Pacific, some six thousand miles from San Francisco. This island would serve as the airbase from which planes would take off to drop the atom bomb on Japan. There on Tinian the components were put together for Little Boy—the uranium gun bomb. Already various sections of the bomb had been delivered by the cruiser *Indianapolis* and three transport planes.

When assembled, the bomb was slightly shorter than a small car—ten feet—but weighed about three times as much, nine thousand pounds. When dropped on Hiroshima, it had the impact of dropping thirteen thousand tons of TNT.

Although the uranium-fueled gun bomb would be the first used on Japan, sections of the Fat Man, or plutonium bomb, were also being flown to Tinian for use in a second bombing if needed. While the first bomb was being assembled, a B-29 crew made a number of practice flights and even dropped a dummy bomb into the sea. Then, on July 27 Truman and the heads of state of Nationalist China and Great Britain issued an ultimatum to Japan, asking for the country's unconditional surrender.

Very quickly, the Japanese prime minister responded, refusing the terms and saying that ". . . there is no other recourse but to ignore it entirely and resolutely fight for the successful conclusion of the war."[1]

The fate of Hiroshima was sealed.

At 2:45 A.M. on August 6, 1945, the *Enola Gay*, a B-29 that had been modified to hold the uranium bomb, took off from Tinian. At 9:14 A.M. the bomb was dropped over Hiroshima. The pilot and crew saw a brilliant flash of light, and then shock waves rolling out of the explosion jolted their plane. Below them they saw dark gray dust split by flashes of fire. It was as if lava or molten molasses had been poured out across the city. A mushroom cloud of purple smoke boiled up forty thousand feet in height.

Estimates of the number who died in the explosion are still in dispute, but the figure is now set at two hundred thousand. More than sixty thousand buildings were destroyed.

The bomb created a hideous hell that author John Hersey would later describe in *Hiroshima*: "Mixed in with the abrasions and lacerations which most people in the hospital had suffered, he began to find dreadful burns. He realized then that casualties were pouring in from outdoors. There were so many that he began to pass up the lightly wounded; he decided that all he could hope to do was to stop people from bleeding to death. Wounded people supported maimed people; disfigured families leaned together. Many people were vomiting."[2]

Rivers and reservoirs were clogged with the bodies of dead people. Hospitals were packed with the injured who could not be treated fast enough. "Patients were dying by the hundreds, but there was nobody to carry away the corpses.

Some of the hospital staff distributed biscuits and rice balls, but the charnel-house smell was so strong that few were hungry."[3]

The victims would soon ask what had created this destruction and how and why they had lucklessly been chosen for its onslaught. "Those scientists who invented the . . . atomic bomb," wrote a woman who was a child at Hiroshima, "what did they think would happen if they dropped it?"[4]

At about 2 P.M. at Los Alamos, Oppenheimer received a phone call from Groves informing him of the drop on Hiroshima. The bomb had gone off "with a tremendous bang," Groves told him.

Oppenheimer replied that everyone at Los Alamos was feeling "reasonably good about it." He congratulated Groves.[5]

He then had his secretary type up an announcement to be read over the Los Alamos public address system.

The physicist Otto Frisch recalled that he heard shouts of glee in the corridor outside his office and went out to find colleagues dashing along the hallways shouting that they had just heard news that the bomb had been dropped on Japan. "It seemed to me that shouts of joy were rather inappropriate," he said.[6]

That same day a giant meeting of clapping and foot-stomping scientists assembled in the Los Alamos theater. Oppenheimer strode proudly down the aisle to address his colleagues. As he got to the podium, he clasped his hands over his head in a victory gesture. That morning at Hiroshima, he told them, the first atomic bomb had blown three-fifths of the city off the face of the earth.

Initially, Oppenheimer had estimated that no more than twenty thousand Japanese would be killed in such a bombing. It was clear that the destruction of human life would far exceed that number.

A victory party was held in one of the men's dormitories but drew only about fifty partygoers. Most talked quietly and sipped drinks as feelings about the day's events began to turn slightly sour. In a corner Oppenheimer was showing a colleague a telex that had arrived from Washington with details of the damage. Both became increasingly upset by the news and soon went home.

As he left the area, Oppenheimer saw a scientist vomiting in the bushes and said to himself, "The reaction has begun."[7] The party inside began to break up by 9 P.M.

U.S. officials had expected Japan to capitulate immediately. Truman's announcement of the bomb had been combined with a new ultimatum for Japan and a warning that the United States might continue to use its powerful new weapon if there was no surrender.

But the devastating "success" of the bomb dropped on Hiroshima actually prolonged the war. It wasn't until the evening of August 6 that Tokyo received word that a small number of enemy planes had nearly destroyed the city with a new type of bomb. It wasn't until August 7 that it was clear that a single bomb had done this damage.

The Japanese cabinet began a series of meetings that ended repeatedly in deadlock. Cabinet ministers were still divided when they heard of the second great catastrophe to strike their nation. On August 10 another atomic bomb, the Fat Man, or implosion bomb, had been dropped on Nagasaki.

When the B-29 took off from Tinian with Fat Man, its primary target had been Kokura Arsenal on the north coast of Kyushu. A secondary target was Nagasaki. But when the plane arrived at Kokura, heavy ground haze and smoke obscured the target. The plane flew on to Nagasaki, but that city was entirely covered with clouds. At the last minute a hole opened in the cloud cover long enough to give the bombardier a chance to drop Fat Man.

Steep hills around the city confined the explosion so that it caused less damage and loss of life, but still one hundred thousand would die.

By then Truman had postponed further bombings until word could be received from the Japanese. Groves in turn had stopped shipments of uranium and plutonium to Tinian. "I did not want to provide any basis for later claims that we had wantonly dropped a third bomb when it was obvious that the war was over," Groves would later write in his memoirs.[8]

On August 10 the Japanese announced that they would accept the terms of the Allied powers provided that the United States would guarantee the survival of the Japanese emperor and his dynasty.

Four days later the victory over Japan was declared, and Los Alamos celebrated, as did the rest of the world. Sirens sounded. Whiskey and gin were taken out of cupboards. Musical comedy and variety shows were put on. George Kistiakowsky, slightly drunk at the time, set off twenty-one cases of TNT in a pyrotechnic display that lit up the whole town of Los Alamos.

But doubts about the jubilation were growing. The wives of the physicists, for example, were at first filled with immense pride in their husbands' achievements, said Laura Fermi, the wife of Enrico Fermi. "When among the praising voices some arose that deprecated the bomb and words like 'barbarism,' 'horror,' 'the crime of Hiroshima,' 'the mass murder,' were heard from several directions, the wives sobered. They wondered, they probed their consciences, but found no answer for their doubts."[9]

Oppenheimer was beginning to feel some of these doubts. He admitted to one of the reporters who visited the laboratory that he was "a little scared of what I have made."[10]

During the week between the bombings of Hiroshima and Nagasaki, Oppenheimer had also worked on a committee at Los Alamos that was supposed to provide advice to the secretary of war on what should be done with the bomb after the war. To those who worked with him he seemed weary and tired and pessimistic about what the future of atomic energy would be. In his report to Secretary of War Henry Stimson he said that the group was sure that even more deadly atomic weapons could be developed and eventually the super, or hydrogen bomb would be built. Oppenheimer also said that the laboratory had been unable to come up with any countermeasure to prevent the delivery of atomic bombs.

It was useless, he said, to think that the United States could remain supreme in the field of atomic weapons for years to come.

"We believe that the safety of this nation . . . cannot lie wholly or even primarily in its scientific or technical prowess. It can be based only on making future wars impossible," Oppenheimer said.[11]

Congratulatory letters and telegrams were flooding in to Los Alamos now that news of the bomb and the scientists who had been working on it was appearing in newspapers. Many of Oppenheimer's old friends wrote to him.

The letters that he wrote in reply to these people reveal more of his fears and hesitancy. He wrote to his old teacher, Herbert Smith, now headmaster of a school in Chicago, that "this undertaking has not been without its misgivings; they are heavy on us today, when the future, which has so many elements of high promise, is yet only a stone's throw from despair."[12]

Oppenheimer, who had been the leader whom all looked up to in the making of the bomb, was now becoming the one that others at Los Alamos looked to for what should happen next. How could this horrible weapon, this monster they had created, be controlled, they wondered.

Because of the friendships he had made in Washington in the course of the building of the bomb, Oppenheimer believed that his role should probably remain one of an adviser, someone who would help the politicians set policy for future use of atomic energy.

But the scientific community wanted some stronger action than that. The physicists and chemists of Los Alamos were particularly upset at the continued pressure from the government to cloak the bomb in secrecy and keep from the public the full story of what it had done to Japan and what would become of it in future.

Within days after Japan's defeat was announced, some five hundred people attended a meeting at the Los Alamos theater to form the Association of Los Alamos Scientists. The group appointed Hans Bethe, Edward Teller, and Frank Oppenheimer to write a statement on the use of the bomb in a future war, the atomic arms race, the feasibility of international control, and the prospects of peacetime application. As Robert Oppenheimer himself noted, much of it mirrored the statements that he had made in his report to Truman's Cabinet.

Almost all civilian workers at the laboratory signed the association statement and then gave it to Oppenheimer, who sent it on to Washington. But the Cabinet decided not to make it public, and Oppenheimer did not push strongly for its release. In fact, he told the association that he felt a group statement would be inadvisable.

His feeling was that public statements about atomic energy would not have as much influence as would the individual advice of scientists such as himself. This angered members of the group because simultaneously other laboratories around the country that had been involved in the making of the bomb had leaked their own statements about atomic energy to the press. Eventually, the Los Alamos statement was reported in the *New York Times*.

Many felt at this point that perhaps Oppenheimer had become too involved with the most influential people in government, so interested in staying close to those with power that he couldn't tell them anything that might make them angry.

The gloomy mood that had settled on Los Alamos contributed to Oppenheimer's feelings that the laboratory should be closed down. He wrote to Groves that he was unsure the laboratory should continue in its present form and that he would like to be relieved of his post as soon as possible. Groves and other government officials wanted the laboratory to continue weapons research, and a replacement, Norris Bradbury, was chosen for Oppenheimer.

Meanwhile, Oppenheimer considered job offers he had received from the universities he had previously been associated with, Cal Tech and the University of California at Berkeley. But he was unsure that he wanted to return to either of these West Coast schools. One problem he had with Berkeley was that during the war years increasing friction had built up between Oppenheimer and his old associate, Ernest Lawrence. Oppenheimer was not sure that he could return to Berkeley, where Lawrence had such a powerful influence, and resume his old role of playing second best on campus to Lawrence. In the end he decided to return to teaching and research at Cal Tech in Pasadena.

Just before he left Los Alamos in October 1945 all of those still at the laboratory gathered for a special ceremony outside Fuller Lodge, one of the old Los Alamos school buildings. General Groves had come to present the laboratory a certificate of appreciation from the army.

Oppenheimer made a speech of acceptance that was to echo for years to come in the minds of the scientists troubled over their discoveries:

It is with appreciation and gratitude that I accept from you this scroll for the Los Alamos Laboratory, for the men and women whose work and whose hearts have made it. It is our hope that in years to come we may look at this scroll, and all that it signifies, with pride.

Today that pride must be tempered with profound concern. If atomic bombs are to be added as new weapons to the arsenals of a warring world, or to the arsenals of nations preparing for war, then the time will come when mankind will curse the names of Los Alamos and Hiroshima.

The peoples of this world must unite or they will perish.

This war, that has ravaged so much of the earth, has written these words. The atomic bomb has spelled them out for all men to understand. Other men have spoken them, in other times, of other wars, of other weapons. They have not prevailed. There are some, misled by a false sense of human history, who hold that they will not prevail today. It is not for us to believe that. By our works we are committed to a world united, before the common peril, in law, and in humanity.[13]

12

"Physics now seems irrelevant"

The end of World War II raised a lot of questions for scientists who had worked on the atomic bomb. Who would control further research on atomic energy: the military community that had controlled Los Alamos or the scientific community that had freely exchanged information on the atom for decades? Would the tight security that had governed atom research during World War II continue after the war? Should the United States share its atom secrets with other nations and could it hope to maintain the monopoly on the atom indefinitely? Should the United States move a giant step further into weapons research and push for development of the hydrogen or H-bomb, the super, that Edward Teller wanted so desperately? Or should there be some kind of world agency, perhaps attached to the United Nations, that would control use of the atom?

Scientists who for years had been locked in the safety of their laboratories and classrooms now found that if they were to have anything to say about these matters they had to get involved in politics. Robert Oppenheimer was at the forefront of those who wanted to have a say in what happened next.

A speech that he gave at Los Alamos in November 1945 to the Association of Los Alamos Scientists revealed how he felt about some of the questions of the day. Afterward, many of the five hundred who heard him would say that they thought he summed up their thoughts and feelings precisely on atomic research.

Atomic weapons had changed forever the nature of war, Oppenheimer said. "I think it is for us to accept it as a very grave crisis," he said, "to realize that these atomic weapons which we have started to make are very terrible, that they involve a change, that they are not just a slight modification."

Even those who knew a lot about bombs "have been slow to understand, slow to believe that the bombs would work, and then slow to understand that their working would present such profound problems," he said.

Oppenheimer urged that all nations participate in a joint atomic energy commission and that there be an exchange of scientists and students among countries. And while all this was going on, he urged, that "no bombs be made."

The United States alone could not expect to control the situation, he said. "However good the motives of this country are . . . we are 140 million people, and there are two billion people living on earth."[1]

After giving that speech Oppenheimer returned to Pasadena and Cal Tech to work on cosmic rays and on studying a tiny subatomic particle called the meson. He would not stay there long. In 1947 he took on a prestigious job in Princeton, New Jersey, as director of the Institute for Advanced Study, a kind of think tank for some of the nation's most brilliant academics in various fields.

But although he had gone back to university life, he was spending very little time on teaching or research. His role in the development of the atom bomb led the president and

Congress to ask him repeatedly for advice on atomic research. "I had a feeling of deep responsibility, interest and concern for many of the problems with which the development of atomic energy confronted our country," he would say later.[2]

But it was more than that, other scientists would say, particularly some of those who disagreed with the ideas he pushed for during this postwar period. He seemed to enjoy his contact with those who held the reins of power, to enjoy the feeling that he had influence over their decisions.

He himself admitted that his role in the bomb project had given him a prominence that few scientists ever gain in the public eye: "I had become widely regarded as a principal author or inventor of the atomic bomb, more widely, I well knew, than the facts warranted. In a modest way I had become a kind of public personage. I was deluged as I have been ever since with requests to lecture and to take part in numerous scientific activities and public affairs."[3]

One of the first controversies that Oppenheimer became involved with in those postwar years was over legislation involving the future administration of nuclear energy. Quite soon after the war Representatives May and Johnson had put together a bill that called for an independent committee to supervise atomic energy. It called for removing atomic energy from the control of the military and would have restored more freedom and independence for researchers.

But the newly formed associations of scientists were upset by its provisions. They felt it was too likely that military officers might get the jobs of administrator and deputy administrator of the new commission and might serve on the committee itself.

They were also upset at fines that the bill would impose on scientists who violated security regulations regarding atomic energy. How could physics professors keep from breaking the security rules in their classrooms and still manage to teach students about the atom?

Supposedly, Oppenheimer had provided advice on the bill as part of a special scientific panel. His fellow scientists were shocked that he was involved with a bill that they felt violated all of the principles of free exchange of information that he had followed all his life.

When he heard about the bill, a young Chicago physicist, Herbert L. Anderson, wrote to a friend: "I must confess my confidence in our own leaders Oppenheimer, Lawrence, Compton, and Fermi, all members of the Scientific Panel . . . who enjoined us to have faith in them and not influence this legislation, is shaken. I believe that these worthy men were duped—that they never had a chance to see this bill. Let us beware of any breach of our rights as men and citizens. The war is won, let us be free again!"[4]

Although Oppenheimer and his friends on the scientific panel were alarmed about some of the security provisions, they felt that they could be revised and that it was important to pass the bill as quickly as possible.

Oppenheimer tried to stave off the opposition of such scientists as Leo Szilard, Harold Urey, and Herbert Anderson. Before Congress he testified that he was sure the president could find a group of intelligent and conscientious men to serve on the commission. He said he didn't fear military domination. The purpose of the May-Johnson bill was to get the army out of the project. He saw it as a way of keeping the momentum going toward some sort of international control for atomic energy.

But Oppenheimer, who had been so capable at molding scientists together to form a team at Los Alamos, was unable to get them to line up behind this legislation. One scientist, Harold Urey, was quoted as calling the bill the "first totalitarian bill ever written by Congress. You can call it either a Communist bill or a Nazi bill, whichever you think is the worse."[5]

Although it may seem hard to believe in light of today's nuclear arms race, in 1946 the United States also pushed for international control of atomic energy. The secretary of state set up a committee headed by Dean Acheson to formulate American policy on the issue. Its members included several people who had worked with Oppenheimer in the past, including Vannevar Bush, James Conant, and Leslie Groves. One of their main jobs was to work with a newly formed United Nations Atomic Energy Commission.

The committee in turn picked an advisory panel headed by David Lilienthal of the Tennessee Valley Authority. Oppenheimer was an enthusiastic member of the advisory panel and already had in mind the outlines of what an international control agency for atomic energy should be like.

Oppenheimer explained to fellow committee members that atomic activities could be classified as either harmless or dangerous. Small reactors, such as those used in university laboratories, were harmless and should not fall under international control. But large reactors for generating nuclear power or for separating uranium 235 were dangerous, large-scale operations that would have to fall under the control of an international authority.

Such an international agency should also have a monopoly on raw materials such a uranium and thorium, he recommended. An agency that knew where mines containing these elements were and controlled their production and sale could detect and discourage illegal enterprises. The international agency should do research on atomic explosives and should develop atomic energy for industrial purposes and power. Only the international agency could operate nuclear power plants. If a country operated its own nuclear power plants, it was believed, it would be too tempting to divert some uranium from the power plants to the making of bombs. If a country broke the international agreement, there would be punishments, although Oppenheimer did not outline what these should be.

In the end the Acheson-Lilienthal committee drew up a

report, most of it based on Oppenheimer's ideas, that was designed to serve as a guide to the first American representative to the United Nations Atomic Energy Commission. The report suggested that the United Nations might serve as the controlling agency for nuclear power throughout the world. It also assumed that Russia would be willing to act in good faith to set up such international controls over atomic energy.

The report was made public and received favorable response. But then the secretary of state appointed Bernard Baruch, a seventy-five-year-old financier, to represent the United States on atomic energy before the United Nations.

Oppenheimer objected to the choice although he didn't say so in public. "That was the day I gave up hope," he said later.[6] He didn't feel that Baruch would be able to resist all of the concessions that Congress and the White House might demand in an international control agency before approaching the Russians with the Acheson-Lilienthal proposal. When Baruch asked Oppenheimer to serve as his chief scientific adviser, he refused.

In the weeks before he went to the United Nations with the proposal for international control, Baruch worked at changing the proposals contained in the report Oppenheimer had worked on. Baruch seemed particularly determined to take a harder line with the Russians than Oppenheimer wanted. He insisted that the international control agency had to fix penalties for criminal actions involving atomic energy, and he also insisted that decisions involving atomic energy had to be decided by majority vote in the United Nations, that no one nation could have veto power, as was currently the case under United Nations rules.

Oppenheimer went to see Truman about Baruch, to express his disappointment with how the report was being changed. He was persuaded to stand by Baruch and to go with him to the United Nations sessions. But at the end of that meeting with the president he made one of those impulsive remarks that would cause him so much trouble in his lifetime. He suddenly blurted out his guilt over the atom bomb project: "Mr. President, I have blood on my hands."

Truman was greatly offended and told Dean Acheson, who had brought Oppenheimer to the meeting, "Don't you bring that fellow around again. After all, all he did was make the bomb. I'm the guy who fired it off."[7]

Oppenheimer later sat on the sidelines at the first meeting of the UN Atomic Energy Commission and watched Baruch present the United States' proposal that it would abolish production of atomic bombs when the commission agreed on conditions for international control. The Russians in turn insisted that the weapons be outlawed first. They refused to consider abolishing their veto power over punishments.

In the end the commission adopted Baruch's proposal, but the Russians abstained from voting. Without Russian participation in the agreement it was meaningless.

At one point David Lilienthal met Oppenheimer in Washington and found him looking depressed and unhappy about the turn of events. "I am ready to go anywhere and do anything," Oppenheimer said, "but I am bankrupt of further ideas. And I find that physics and the teaching of physics, which is my life, now seems irrelevant."[8]

In 1947 Oppenheimer resigned as science adviser to the UN Atomic Energy Commission and thus admitted to himself that international control was a hopeless cause.

Meanwhile, the combined forces of Congress, scientists, and even some White House officials had succeeded in blocking the May-Johnson bill. Now new legislation was brought forward by Senator Brien McMahon of Connecticut. This bill set up an Atomic Energy Commission controlled by civilians. The legislation promised more freedom for research even though it still allowed the military to take over atomic research in times of national emergency.

Appointed as the first chairman of the commission was

David Lilienthal, who had worked with Oppenheimer on the international atomic energy proposal. Another member was Robert Bacher, a friend of Oppenheimer's. The commission in turn picked a scientific panel, known as the General Advisory Committee, made up of Oppenheimer and several of his former associates and friends: Isidor Rabi, Enrico Fermi, James Conant, John Manley, and Lee DuBridge.

Oppenheimer arrived late for the first meeting of the group only to find that he had been elected chairman. Once again he had the chance to serve as a leader, to influence decision making, to speak fluently and eloquently as only he could do.

The group usually met over three-day weekends when the panel members could get away from their other jobs. At the end of their sessions, when Atomic Energy Commission members came in to review their work, Oppenheimer would summarize the proceedings for them. "This was Oppenheimer at his very best," said Glenn Seaborg, who was a member of the General Advisory Committee at one point. "I regret that tape recordings were not made of these eloquent summations of our deliberations, for these were better than the written record that followed and would provide fascinating historical material."[9]

In those days on the committee Oppenheimer worked for peaceful uses of the atom and continued support for researchers. "He saw the dawn of a new age of science and knew that the government's relationship to science would never be the same," Seaborg said.[10]

That doesn't mean that Oppenheimer wasn't still involved with weapons research. The committee also gave advice on continued research and development of atomic weapons and the use of carriers, aircraft, and missiles involving atom bombs. Members also pushed for development of atomic reactors that could serve as a power source for submarines and other navy vessels.

Finally, Oppenheimer seemed to have found a role for himself that would work, a chance to express opinions and influence policy in a group that respected and looked up to him.

But although he continued to be respected and admired, to receive honors and plaudits, stormy forces were beginning to gather that would create great trials in future. Some of it was of his own making: His past involvement with Communist front groups and his ability to make enemies with his sharp tongue and sometimes manipulative manner were part of the cause. Some of it was beyond his control: the fact that Russia would soon have its own atomic bomb and the shock waves that this would send through Congress and the White House.

13

"The best security is in the grave"

Although Oppenheimer was discouraged by the progress of his hopes for worldwide controls over atomic energy, the first few years after World War II held other rewards. First there was his new job at the Institute for Advanced Study at Princeton. Before his arrival many famous physicists had joined the institute, including Albert Einstein, but Oppenheimer set about further enhancing the quality and reputation of the institute as a center for physics and mathematics. He brought in several dynamic young research associates who had worked with him in California.

In Princeton, Oppenheimer and Kitty lived with Peter and Toni at Olden Manor, a spacious white frame house on the institute grounds. Their walls were hung with the collection of paintings that Oppenheimer had inherited from his parents, including a Van Gogh. Oppenheimer himself never added to the collection, but he enjoyed showing it to others. The new home was large enough to provide a library for Oppenheimer, a greenhouse for his wife, a photographic studio for Peter, and for Toni a stall for a pony.

The Oppenheimers' parties drew a mixture of prominent political, scientific, and artistic guests, to whom Oppenheimer served the martinis for which he became famous.

Although Oppenheimer was sometimes criticized for being an uncaring father, wrapped up in his career and politics, there were warm moments in his relationship with his children. One friend told of having been at the Oppenheimers' and seeing Peter Oppenheimer and his mother, Kitty, engrossed in trying to get a homemade toy, "the gimmick," to work. The "gimmick" was a board with lights, buzzers, and other devices on one side and fuses, wires, and switches underneath. When Kitty was called to the kitchen, Oppenheimer sat down on the floor to struggle with the wiring while his dinner guests watched. Peter rushed into the kitchen to ask his mother, "Is it all right to let Daddy work with the gimmick?"[1]

Awards and honors poured in for Oppenheimer, from being named Father of the Year by the National Baby Institution to being chosen for the Hall of Fame of the First Half of the Century by the magazine *Popular Mechanics*. More serious distinctions included the Medal of Merit he received from President Truman. In 1953 he also received his sixth doctorate, an honorary one from Oxford University in England.

But all the while a time bomb out of Oppenheimer's past ticked away—his links to Communist-sponsored groups. As the Cold War intensified and anti-Communist feeling grew in the United States, the associations that Oppenheimer and his relatives had once had with left-wing groups looked increasingly suspicious to those who feared Russia and Russia's power.

First, in March 1947 FBI Director J. Edgar Hoover sent a report about the past radical activities of Robert and Frank Oppenheimer to David Lilienthal of the Atomic Energy Commission, just before the commission was to vote on Oppenheimer's security clearance. The report discussed how Robert Oppenheimer had belonged to various Communist front organizations and had hired known Communists at the Berkeley Radiation Laboratory. The report also touched on the Haakon Chevalier incident.

The material shocked Lilienthal, but it also puzzled him. Why had Hoover decided to raise these issues after all of the years that Oppenheimer had had access to the nation's most confidential secrets? Was it simply part of the nationwide scare campaign over communism? he wondered.

Lilienthal called a special commission meeting to which longtime friends of Oppenheimer were summoned: General Groves, Vannevar Bush, and James Conant. All vouched for Oppenheimer's loyalty. Although the report looked ominous, the deputy general counsel for the commission, Joseph Volpe, reported that very little in the file indicated that Oppenheimer was a security risk. The commission agreed and voted to give Oppenheimer a security clearance.

Then, in 1947 a Washington newspaper, the *Times Herald*, ran a story reporting that Oppenheimer's brother, Frank, was a one-time member of the Communist Party and had worked on the A-bomb. Even so, the newspaper also ran this disclaimer: "The *Times Herald* wishes to emphasize that the official report on Frank Oppenheimer in no way reflects on the loyalty or ability of his brother, Dr. J. Robert Oppenheimer."[2]

But the pressure over hunting out past Communists was building, and in 1949 the House Un-American Activities Committee began an investigation of past activities of Communists at the Berkeley Radiation Laboratory. It was inevitable that eventually Oppenheimer was called.

In June 1949 Oppenheimer appeared before the committee to answer questions about some of his former students, Rossi Lomanitz, Joseph Weinberg, and others. Next he was asked about his kitchen conversation with Haakon Chevalier, the one that had occurred in the early months of the Los Alamos project. His reply defended Chevalier: "Dr. Chevalier was clearly embarrassed and confused, and I, in violent terms, told him not to be confused and to have no connection with it. He did not ask me for information."[3]

Oppenheimer was asked if he reported the incident to the Manhattan District security officers, but no one brought up the fact that he waited eight months to do so. He denied that he had been a Communist as well. But then someone asked him about his brother's membership in the Communist Party, and Oppenheimer begged for permission not to answer. The commission withdrew the question without hesitation.

All in all, the session went very smoothly, and Oppenheimer seemed to have charmed the commissioners, including one congressman, Richard Nixon, who said that he had been "tremendously impressed" with Oppenheimer and was "mighty happy" that Oppenheimer was at work in the nation's atomic energy program.

A few days later, however, Oppenheimer was part of another hearing, which did not go as smoothly and again showed how easy it was for him to alienate others because of his brilliance and witty sarcasm. The occasion this time was an investigation by the Joint Congressional Committee on Atomic Energy of a charge that the brand-new Atomic Energy Commission was being mismanaged. The charges stemmed partly from friction between various branches of the armed forces and the Atomic Energy Commission over who would control atomic weapons.

Oppenheimer was called in because of questions about the exporting of radioactive isotopes to foreign researchers. Some on the commission felt this was a dubious practice. In particular, Oppenheimer clashed with Commissioner Lewis Strauss, a man who had made a fortune on Wall Street but who had also served as an admiral during World War II.

In his objections Strauss noted that in one case an isotope had been sent to a Norwegian research group that included a Communist among its members. While Oppenheimer was on the witness stand, Strauss asked him about possible military uses of the isotopes. In other words, couldn't someone who had applied to get quantities of an isotope for a lab experiment actually end up using it to build a bomb?

Of course it was a possibility, Oppenheimer said. "You can use a shovel for atomic energy," he went on. "In fact you do. You can use a bottle of beer for atomic energy. In fact you do."

As the audience tittered, Strauss seemed visibly upset. His anger at Oppenheimer's arrogance was written on his face. He was a man who didn't enjoy being the brunt of a joke.

"The best guarding is simply to lock everything up and not let anybody in," Oppenheimer went on. "The best security is in the grave."

After the hearing Oppenheimer asked a friend how he'd done. "Too well, Robert," was the reply. "Much too well."[4]

The very next day Frank Oppenheimer appeared before the House Un-American Activities Committee with his wife, and both of them admitted to having belonged to the Communist Party. But they said they had left the party in 1940 before Frank had gone to work at Los Alamos.

An hour later Frank Oppenheimer learned that the University of Minnesota was asking him to resign his post as an assistant professor of physics. In spite of his service at Los Alamos and the commendations he had earned, Frank's career in physics had been cut short. He retired to some land he had bought in Colorado to raise cattle. It was a sad blow for the Oppenheimers, and Robert Oppenheimer must have wondered what his brother's fate might mean to him.

Just a year later, in May 1950, a Mrs. Sylvia Crouch appeared before a separate committee on un-American activities that had been set up in California. Before that group, she testified that she and her husband had attended a meeting of top-drawer Communist leaders at which Oppenheimer served as host. It had been a closed, special meeting, she said, that even ordinary Communists were not notified about.

Twice in a week the FBI interviewed Oppenheimer about these allegations, but he had a firm alibi. The meeting in question took place shortly after his son was born. His wife's illness following the birth would have kept him from participating in meetings of any kind, he said. Around the time he was supposed to have been at the meeting, he said, he was on a holiday in New Mexico with Kitty, who had been recuperating from Peter's birth.

Behind the scenes the intrigue continued. William Liscum Borden, the executive director of the Joint Congressional Committee on Atomic Energy, the group that had been investigating mismanagement at the Atomic Energy Commission, had growing suspicions about Oppenheimer. In November 1950 he asked the Atomic Energy Commission to provide him with the files of the employees who had been the commission's biggest security cases. One of the files he received was that of Robert Oppenheimer.

14

"Keep your shirt on"

During the first years after World War II the prospect of an even bigger bomb—the H-bomb, or super—also cast a shadow over Oppenheimer's life. He would one day be called to account for almost every word and action involving this bigger, more frightening bomb, which, it was predicted, would have the strength of 10 million tons of TNT.

All through the Manhattan Project, Edward Teller, who had clashed with Oppenheimer so many times at Los Alamos, had continued to work on a design for the hydrogen bomb. In the atomic bomb energy is released when the nuclei of atoms are split. The theory behind the hydrogen bomb was that energy would be released when small nuclei fuse to form a larger nucleus.

Originally, Teller had been asked to stay on at Los Alamos as head of the physics department, but he declined to do so when laboratory leaders seemed uncertain about whether they would put in the major effort on the hydrogen bomb that he wanted. So Teller decided to return at least temporarily to the University of Chicago to do research and teaching.

When Teller informed Oppenheimer of his decision, Oppenheimer told him, "Our accomplishments in Los Alamos have been remarkable, and it will be a long time before anyone can improve on them." Teller was upset about that. "I felt less optimistic and could not agree with Oppie's attitude," he wrote later.[1]

While Oppenheimer was off making friends and enemies in Washington and working on his plans for international control of atomic energy, Teller kept pushing his idea for the hydrogen bomb. In April 1946 Teller went back to Los Alamos to head a secret conference on the H-bomb. The formula that Teller had roughed out called for putting together an atomic bomb, a cubic meter of liquid deuterium, and an indefinite amount of the rare isotope of hydrogen, tritium.

The conference decided that Teller's recipe for the H-bomb could work, although some of those at the meeting had doubts. The group concluded that mathematical studies should continue but that before the bomb could be built, the government would have to make a tremendous investment of resources and manpower.

All this time U.S. officials had been wondering how long it might be before Russia developed an atomic bomb of its own. Then, in September 1949 a U.S. Air Force plane on a scientific mission in the Far East detected radioactivity in the atmosphere and in rainwater. What they found, scientists determined, could only have come from an atomic explosion somewhere in Soviet Asia.

Oppenheimer was at Princeton at the time. "I had just got into the house," he said, "when I heard the phone ringing. It was to tell me that our surveillance network had picked up evidence that the Russians had detonated an A-bomb."[2]

American officials couldn't believe that their monopoly over the atomic bomb had been broken by what they soon nicknamed Joe I, in "honor" of the Russian dictator Joseph Stalin. Everyone had trusted predictions that the Russians could not put together a bomb until 1956 or possibly 1960. How had they managed to produce enough uranium 235 or plutonium so quickly? Some felt that spies must have smuggled the fissionable material to Russia.

President Truman called Oppenheimer to Washington to ask him if he thought the news of the bomb was true. Truman wasn't thoroughly convinced, even though Oppenheimer assured him that a Russian bomb was possible and urged that the American people be informed about it.

Oppenheimer was also summoned to a secret congressional hearing to discuss the news. When senators and representatives asked him what the country should do next, he told the group: "Stay strong and hold on to our friends."[3]

When Truman finally made a public announcement about the Russian bomb test, Teller, of course, was seized with a new fervor for the H-bomb. Perhaps now the outside world would pay attention to his idea. He called up Oppenheimer to ask, "What shall we do?"

"Keep your shirt on" was Oppenheimer's advice.[4]

But others besides Teller were upset and impatient with Oppenheimer's advice that the nation shouldn't panic over the Russian bomb. Within days after Truman's announcement Ernest Lawrence and another former Manhattan Project scientist, Luis Alvarez, had flown to Los Alamos to talk to Teller about the super and to ask what should be done to produce this bigger bomb that would trump the Russian discovery. "It occurred to me that the Russians might be working hard on a super of their own and might succeed in building that potentially vastly more destructive weapon before we did. The only practical defense against such an eventuality seemed to be to get there first," Luis Alvarez said.[5]

Lewis Strauss had also written to his fellow members on the Atomic Energy Commission to urge them to "make an intensive effort to get ahead with the super,"[6] an effort that he said should be comparable to the one that went into building the first atomic bomb.

The commission chairman, David Lilienthal, was less enthusiastic than Strauss. After all, weapons researchers by then had already built a new atomic bomb that was twenty-five times as powerful as the bomb that was dropped on Hiroshima. Why was anything bigger than that needed? But he called on Oppenheimer and other members of the General Advisory Committee to hold a special meeting at the end of October.

Meanwhile, Teller pushed hard to recruit scientists to return to Los Alamos, even though it was clear that there were serious technical obstacles to overcome before the super could be built. In a few months one scientist working on the project would determine that such a large amount of tritium would be necessary as an ingredient in the bomb that it would be too costly to produce.

Oppenheimer was well aware of the questions about Teller's design. He even wrote a fellow member of the General Advisory Committee, James Conant: "I am not sure the miserable thing will work, nor that it can be gotten to a target except by ox cart."

He also questioned whether it would solve the nation's growing problems with Russia or just make them worse. "That we become committed to it as the way to save the country and the peace appears to me full of dangers," he said.

But still he took what is often the typical scientist's approach—if there is something scientific to investigate, it should be done regardless of the political consequences. It was the same approach that fueled the research on the original atomic bomb. "It would be folly to oppose the exploration of this weapon. We have always known it had to be done; and it does have to be done, though it appears to be singularly proof against any form of experimental approach," Oppenheimer wrote.[7]

During his recruiting process Teller contacted Hans Bethe, who had become a professor at Cornell University in Ithaca, New York, and asked him to return to Los Alamos to work on the H-bomb. Bethe was tempted to go, particularly since the researchers would be using the newest in electronic computers, which were then restricted to military projects.

But like Oppenheimer, Bethe had doubts about what an H-bomb would mean to the world: "It seemed to me that the development of thermonuclear weapons would not solve any of the difficulties that we found ourselves in and yet I was not quite sure whether I should refuse."[8]

While talking to Teller about what he should do, Bethe received a phone call from Oppenheimer. Teller felt that Bethe was upset after talking to Oppenheimer and was worried when Bethe said he wanted to visit Oppenheimer to talk about the super. "We are going to talk with Oppenheimer," Teller predicted, "and then you will not come!"[9]

So Teller and Bethe went to Princeton and met with Oppenheimer in his office. For the most part, at that session Oppenheimer refrained from giving many of his own views about the hydrogen bomb. Instead he talked about James Conant, who, he said, strongly opposed the hydrogen bomb project. Oppenheimer himself urged that if an H-bomb were to be developed, there shouldn't be the same tight secrecy surrounding the research as had cloaked the A-bomb at Los Alamos.

After they left Oppenheimer, Bethe assured Teller: "You see you can be quite satisfied. I am still coming."[10]

But Bethe's doubts grew, and after conversations with other close friends he changed his mind and backed out of going to Los Alamos. Although he had no firm proof, Teller was sure that Oppenheimer must have played a role in Bethe's decision.

Then, on October 29, 1949, as rain dampened the streets of Washington, D.C., the General Advisory Committee and Atomic Energy Commission met at the commission headquarters to give their views on whether the United States should embark on producing a thermonuclear bomb.

During the morning the committee heard from military heroes such as General of the Army Omar Bradley on what the Soviet bomb meant to the nation. Bradley advised that the nation had no choice but to build the H-bomb.

At lunchtime Oppenheimer ate with Robert Serber of the commission and Luis Alvarez, who was in Washington to lobby for the building of the super. Oppenheimer told Alvarez he didn't think the United States should build the hydrogen bomb. "The main reason he gave was that if we built a hydrogen bomb then the Russians would build a hydrogen bomb, whereas if we didn't build a hydrogen bomb then the Russians wouldn't build a hydrogen bomb," Alvarez said. "I thought this point of view odd and incomprehensible. I told Robert that he might find his argument reassuring but that I doubted if he would find many Americans who would accept it."[11]

After lunch Oppenheimer asked each member of the committee to give his opinion on the bomb. All nine members were present except for Glenn Seaborg, chemist from the University of California at Berkeley, who was on a trip to Sweden.

The various speakers commented on whether the H-bomb was feasible and how it would expand the arsenal of weapons that the United States already had. If the nation already had enough powerful bombs, did it need a bigger one?

The tide seemed to be turning against the H-bomb. As Oppenheimer later put it: "There was a surprising unanimity . . . that the United States ought not to take the initiative at that time in an all-out program for the development of thermo-nuclear weapons."[12]

After everyone spoke, Oppenheimer said he was glad that the discussion had turned out as it had because otherwise "I would have had to resign as chairman."[13]

But Oppenheimer had either forgotten or overlooked one important matter. Before the meeting he had received a letter from Glenn Seaborg, whose views did not exactly match those of the rest of the committee. Seaborg's letter said that although he "deplored" seeing the United States put a tremendous effort into building the H-bomb, nevertheless "I must confess that I have been unable to come to the conclusion that we should not."[14] Oppenheimer neglected to read the letter to the committee, a mistake for which he would pay later.

For the next two days the advisory committee drafted its report. The main conclusion was "We are all agreed that it would be wrong at the present moment to commit ourselves to an all-out effort towards its development."[15]

The group argued that the H-bomb didn't make much sense in terms of warfare. What sort of target was it good for? the panel asked. And what would be the general political effect?

In other words, if the military pinpointed a target and then dropped an H-bomb on it, the bomb would knock out much more than the target, much more than military leaders aimed to destroy. The report urged that the nation instead should work on developing fission bombs and learning to use them effectively.

Two committee members, Isidor Rabi and Enrico Fermi, went even further than the rest of the group, including Oppenheimer. "The application of this weapon with the consequent great release of radioactivity would have results unforeseeable at present," the two wrote, "but would certainly render large areas unfit for habitation for long periods of time." They concluded: "It is necessarily an evil thing considered in any light."[16]

A short time later the Atomic Energy Commission itself took up the question of the super, but at first its members couldn't arrive at a consensus. They decided to report to the president individually on the matter. David Lilienthal and one other commissioner were opposed to building the fusion bomb. Two other commissioners favored trying to make an agreement with the Russians before launching a crash H-bomb program. Lewis Strauss, fast becoming Oppenheimer's enemy, favored the bomb. Eventually, two other commissioners changed their minds and swung to Strauss's point of view.

Strauss pushed hard and lobbied the secretary of defense and other Washington officials. Various senators lined up behind Teller and the H-bomb cause. Other pressure groups worked behind the scenes as well, including members of the military and a number of scientists who disagreed with Oppenheimer, such as Ernest Lawrence and Edward Teller.

In spite of intense lobbying, most of it being done by supporters of the super, for two months Truman held off making a commitment to the bomb project. Then, on January 27, 1950, Klaus Fuchs, the refugee scientist who had worked for Oppenheimer at Los Alamos, confessed to police in London that he had for many years been communicating to the Russians all of the atomic secrets to which he had access. Many estimated that the information that Fuchs passed to the Russians enabled them to cut several years off the research needed to build Joe I.

Although news of the espionage did not become public until February, Truman reacted swiftly on the H-bomb. On January 31 the president announced: "I have directed the Atomic Energy Commission to continue its work on all forms of atomic weapons, including the so-called hydrogen or super-bomb."[17]

Later that same day Lewis Strauss held a party to celebrate his fifty-fourth birthday and the president's announcement about the H-bomb. Oppenheimer attended, although he was feeling morose and downcast over the whole affair.

A fellow guest approached him and asked why he looked so upset. "This is the plague of Thebes," Oppenheimer replied.[18] That was not the end of Oppenheimer's role in the development of the H-bomb. Nor did Truman's decision to move ahead with the project mean that Teller and Los Alamos were able to produce the super efficiently and quickly.

Early in 1950 Dr. Stanislaw Ulam, who was working on

the super project with Teller, discovered that most of the early calculations that Teller had made were wrong. When Teller heard the news, he went "pale with fury," Ulam told an associate at the time.[19] It seemed to prove one of Oppenheimer's own conclusions about the super: Scientists did not yet have enough knowledge to embark on an adventurous and expensive crash program for this new bomb.

The problem with the super resembled the one that Oppenheimer had faced at Los Alamos in building an atomic bomb. The fission bomb that set fusion off inside the super had to move at incredible speeds, almost the speed of light, or it would blow the bomb apart before fusion could take place. Nevertheless, Teller and fellow scientists at Los Alamos moved ahead. By early 1951 they had found a solution.

In June 1950 an Atomic Energy Commission and the General Advisory Committee met in Princeton to discuss progress on the super. Teller and various Los Alamos officials were invited to attend. A few days beforehand Teller explained his new formula to Oppenheimer and found him enthusiastic about his solution to the H-bomb problem. Yet neither Oppenheimer nor anyone else put Teller on the agenda to speak. Teller grew increasingly furious as the meeting progressed and finally dashed to the front of the room to chalk out his formulas on the blackboard.

As soon as he finished, Oppenheimer and others at the meeting commented warmly on Teller's approach. He and others at the meeting went on to recommend that Teller's group push ahead on the hydrogen bomb and that they set up a schedule for testing the device. Oppenheimer's change of heart seemed like a complete reversal of everything he had fought for in the past few years.

Why did Oppenheimer's objections evaporate once Teller showed that the super could be made? Partly, it seems to have been due to his conviction as a scientist that whatever can be done must be done. Partly, it seemed to be the feeling that the nation could only outlaw this weapon before it had been created. Once a way had been found to build it, the project had to move ahead.

Oppenheimer said later: "When I saw how to do it, it was clear to me that one had to at least make the thing. Then the only problem was what would one do about them when one had them. The program we had in 1949 was a tortured thing that you could well argue did not make a great deal of technical sense. It was therefore possible to argue also that you did not want it even if you could have it. The program in 1951 was technically so sweet that you could not argue about that. It was purely the military, the political and the humane problem of what you were going to do about it once you had it."[20]

After that, only time stood in the way. On November 1, 1952, "Mike," the hydrogen bomb, was tested at the Eniwetok Atoll in the South Pacific. The yield of the bomb was estimated at 10.4 million tons of TNT, a thousand times more violent than the Little Boy or Thin Man bomb that fell on Japan. The entire one-mile island of Elugelab, where the bomb had been detonated, disappeared.

15

"Like Pearl Harbor on a small scale"

In November 1953 William Borden, the man who had been studying Oppenheimer's files, was almost ready to leave his job with the Joint Congressional Committee on Atomic Energy to take a post in private industry. But as a final act he put together his charges against Robert Oppenheimer in a detailed and well-researched letter and sent them to the director of the Federal Bureau of Investigation, J. Edgar Hoover.

Borden had taken a number of incidents in Oppenheimer's life and had tried to weave them together to form a pattern of guilt, to create a picture of Oppenheimer as a Soviet agent who had spied for the Russians.

The letter pointed out many of the past associations of Oppenheimer and his family with Communists, evidence that Oppenheimer had never denied and that several investigative officials and groups had looked at before. Borden also noted that during the war he hired a number of Communists at Los Alamos.

Many of Borden's accusations related to the opinions that

Oppenheimer had had about the building of the hydrogen bomb.

For example, he said:

"He [Oppenheimer] was remarkably instrumental in influencing the military authorities and the Atomic Energy Commission essentially to suspend H-bomb development from mid-1946 through January 31, 1950.

"He has worked tirelessly, from January 31, 1950 [when Truman announced work on the H-bomb], onward, to retard the United States H-bomb program.

"He has used his potent influence against every major postwar effort toward atomic power development, including the nuclear-powered submarine and aircraft programs as well as industrial power projects."

On the basis of all of these statements, Borden reached a dramatic and alarming conclusion about Oppenheimer that seemed to many people to go beyond the facts he had started with. He concluded that from 1939 on Oppenheimer had been an espionage agent for the Soviets and had "acted under a Soviet directive in influencing United States military, atomic energy, intelligence and diplomatic policy."[1]

Borden also alleged that, on the basis of information furnished by the spy Klaus Fuchs, Oppenheimer might have been the Communist agent in Berkeley who informed the Russians about electromagnetic separation research during 1942 or earlier.

Although these allegations were stronger than anything that had been said before about Oppenheimer, some of them summed up material that had been heatedly discussed for several years.

Senator Joseph McCarthy, who had launched investigations of alleged Communists in government through a special Senate Investigations Subcommittee, had once contemplated a probe of Oppenheimer. He had been discouraged by Lewis Strauss and J. Edgar Hoover. Although Hoover and Strauss didn't like Oppenheimer, they felt that the case against Oppenheimer was not strong enough yet to justify action.

But Hoover and the FBI maintained surveillance of Oppenheimer in the postwar years, including interviewing his associates, such as Edward Teller. At one point one of the AEC commissioners had even declared that Oppenheimer was a security risk and should be removed.

Perhaps because of all of that pressure, when Oppenheimer came up for reelection as chairman of the General Advisory Committee to the Atomic Energy Commission in the summer of 1952, he declined to continue on the committee. But he still remained a consultant with a contract to work for the commission. Even the contract irritated Strauss, who took over as chairman of the Atomic Energy Commission in 1953, but he decided to hold out until the contract came up for renewal in 1954.

Oppenheimer's friends and protectors in Washington found it increasingly difficult to shield him from the attacks of his enemies. In May 1953, for example, there was a new attack on Oppenheimer in the press via an unsigned article published in the business magazine *Fortune*. The title of the article was "The Hidden Struggle for the H-Bomb: The Story of Dr. Oppenheimer's Persistent Campaign to Reverse U.S. Military Strategy."

The article later turned out to have been written by an air force reserve officer who had close associations with many other high-ranking officers in the service. Much of it focused on conflicts between a small group of American scientists, led by Oppenheimer, and the Strategic Air Command. According to the writer, the scientists hoped to use an air-defense system to make nuclear weapons redundant. The scientists' actions were interpreted as an attempt to block the building of the super, or H-bomb.

With all of this as background, it seemed inevitable that eventually someone like Borden would develop a detailed case against Oppenheimer. The FBI spent about three weeks looking at Borden's charges and then sent them on to President Dwight Eisenhower. Eisenhower, like Truman before him, was under pressure from anti-Communist political groups, who claimed that the federal bureaucracy was loaded with Communist sympathizers. Regardless of how he might have felt personally about the charges against Oppenheimer, Eisenhower decided to take action.

First he held a meeting to discuss the charges with some cabinet members and Lewis Strauss. The upshot was that Eisenhower suspended Oppenheimer's security clearance. In effect, he ordered a blank wall placed between Oppenheimer and all government secrets.

Then the Atomic Energy Commission met and agreed to hold an inquiry on the charges. This in itself was not unusual because the commission held many boards of inquiry every year to decide on the security clearance of employees. Usually these hearings were informal sessions of about an hour, mainly aimed at clearing someone. Generally, there were no lawyers, and the rules of evidence followed in courtrooms did not apply in the hearings.

Unaware of the storm that was raging over his career, Oppenheimer had gone to England to receive an honorary degree and to deliver a series of important lectures. When he returned to Princeton, he was summoned to Washington for an emergency meeting with Strauss and the general manager of the Atomic Energy Commission, K. D. Nichols, who had previously served as an assistant to General Leslie Groves.

On December 21 Strauss handed Oppenheimer the list of charges. Oppenheimer looked over the document prepared by the Atomic Energy Commission staff and found that most of it centered on his past dealings with Communists. But the statement also indicated that he had strongly opposed the building of the hydrogen bomb both before and after President Truman had ordered it built. The letter raised questions as to

Oppenheimer's "veracity, conduct and even loyalty." Oppenheimer commented that some charges were incorrectly stated, some he would deny, and others were correct.[2]

In the back of everyone's mind at the meeting was the question of whether Oppenheimer would back down and resign. The idea was discussed, but there was always confusion about who first brought up the suggestion that he quit. In later years Oppenheimer would claim that Strauss suggested it; others at the meeting insisted that Oppenheimer asked if he should resign.

At any rate, Nichols told Oppenheimer that if he quit there would be no security hearing because Oppenheimer would no longer be a government employee. Strauss gave Oppenheimer a day to think about the possibilities and to decide if he would resign.

Although Oppenheimer had faced accusations about his past before, the events of that day seemed to come as a surprise. Looking back on the incident later in life, Oppenheimer said, "It was like Pearl Harbor . . . on a small scale. Given the circumstances and the spirit of the times, one knew that something like this was possible and even probable; but still it was a shock when it came."[3]

Before making his decision Oppenheimer and his wife, Kitty, sat down with friends and an attorney for a discussion, which lasted from late in the afternoon until nearly midnight, about the alternatives open to him.

Why should he face the hearing when there was less than a year remaining on his government contract? On the other hand, if he didn't have a hearing under the Atomic Energy Commission, it was possible that Senator Joseph McCarthy might single him out for a Senate hearing, one in which he might have less chance to defend himself. If he resigned, would he look guilty in the eyes of the public even though nothing had been proved against him? Would the Atomic Energy Commission leak the charges against him to the press? And hadn't he succeeded in the past in refuting accusations brought against him? During World War II, after all, he had managed to get a security clearance in spite of charges about his membership in Communist front groups. The next day Oppenheimer and Kitty went to Strauss's office to announce that they would undergo the hearing.

Although the Christmas season was in full swing, the Oppenheimers had some surprising visitors at their home in Princeton on Christmas Eve. Two representatives of the Atomic Energy Commission arrived to pick up all of the secret commission documents that Oppenheimer kept in his office.

During the next few months the two sides marshaled their forces and evidence. On the face of it, it seemed that Oppenheimer would have a strong chance in spite of the anti-Communist feeling sweeping the nation. His intellectual brilliance and charm had helped ease him through tight situations before.

But from the start Oppenheimer's forces seemed awkward and confused, unsure of how to put together his case. Not only that, the other side also had an advantage that Oppenheimer and his defenders were unaware of. Beginning in January 1954 the FBI had installed bugging and wiretapping equipment in Oppenheimer's home. His every move took place under the watchful eye of the FBI, and much of his defense was revealed to federal officials.

One of Oppenheimer's first acts was to choose a lawyer. His choice was a distinguished one: Lloyd Garrison, a former University of Wisconsin law school dean and a descendant of the famous Civil War–era abolitionist William Lloyd Garrison. But as distinguished as Garrison was, he was known as a mild-mannered intellectual and had little courtroom experience.

Meanwhile, it was becoming clear that the security hearing would not be informal in tone, as previous ones had been, but would be turned into a trial, although such hearing panels had no validity as a court of law. Even before a hearing board was chosen, Strauss hunted for an outside attorney with extensive trial experience to serve as prosecutor. The choice was Roger Robb, a man with seven years experience as an assistant U.S. attorney, who had tried twenty-three murder cases and other criminal cases.

The next difficulty for the group working on behalf of Oppenheimer was the question of security clearances. Because the hearing would involve so much top-secret material, anyone working on the case needed to get a security clearance in order to look into all of the matters Oppenheimer had been involved with.

Within eight days Robb was granted an emergency security clearance, and he spent the next two months sitting in his office sifting through piles of documents. Due to a snafu on the part of Garrison and some other attorneys helping him with the case, Garrison failed to ask for a security clearance until about seventeen days before the hearing was to start. Although a clearance had been rushed through for Robb, the commission said it could not do the same for Garrison. When the hearing ended, eight weeks after Garrison's request, he still had not gotten his clearance.

So while Robb could call up any government document he wished, including tapes of the ten-year-old interviews that the security officials had with Oppenheimer about Haakon Chevalier, Garrison's requests were refused. While working on Oppenheimer's defense, Garrison and Oppenheimer were forced to depend primarily on Oppenheimer's memories of the past.

By early March, Oppenheimer had put together a forty-two-page reply to the commission's charges. For the most part, however, it was a detailed biography rather than a point-by-point rebuttal. In an accompanying letter, he said he had written his reply in this way because "the items of so-called derogatory information set forth in your letter cannot be fairly understood except in the context of my life and my work."[4]

In closing, Oppenheimer said: "In preparing this letter,

I have reviewed two decades of my life. I have recalled instances where I acted unwisely. What I have hoped was, not that I could wholly avoid error, but that I might learn from it. What I have learned has, I think made me more fit to serve my country."[5]

Shortly before the hearing, set for April 12, the members of the hearing board were chosen. To pick them, the Atomic Energy Commission combed the country to find a panel as distinguished as Oppenheimer himself.

The chairman of the hearing board was Gordon Gray, the forty-five-year-old president of the University of North Carolina and descendant of a wealthy family. The others were Thomas Alfred Morgan, board chairman of the Sperry Corporation and on the board of directors of a number of major companies and banks, and Ward V. Evans, chairman of the Northwestern University chemistry department and a man known as a conservative Republican.

If Oppenheimer had actually faced a courtroom trial, he would have had a jury who had to start from scratch on the evidence. Everything they would learn about the case they would learn in the courtroom setting. But in this case prosecutor Robb spent a week briefing the hearing panelists on what was to come. When they took their places in the hearing room, each had a thick black notebook of material from government files and investigative reports supplied by Robb.

So on the one hand, Oppenheimer was going to be prosecuted as if he were in a courtroom. On the other hand, he would have none of the protections that shield the accused in the nation's courtrooms.

16

"In the matter of J. Robert Oppenheimer"

On April 12, 1954, the hearing "in the matter of J. Robert Oppenheimer" opened at 10 A.M. in a broad, oblong room in the Atomic Energy Commission's Building T-3 in Washington, D.C. A row of windows looked out onto the lawn of the Ellipse just south of the White House. At one end of the room a table had been set up for the hearing board members. At other tables sat the attorneys for the Atomic Energy Commission, Garrison and other attorneys, and Robert Oppenheimer. There was a lone "witness chair" and also a leather sofa where Oppenheimer would sit to watch the proceedings when he wasn't testifying himself. For the next four weeks, the group would gather almost daily to review the details of Oppenheimer's life almost from his birth, including both his triumphs and his failures, his successes and his mistakes.

The first day began with the reading of charges against Oppenheimer and of his reply. Chairman Gordon Gray warned those present that the proceedings "are regarded as strictly confidential" between the commission and Oppenheimer and that the hearing should not be regarded as a trial.[1]

But the warning about secrecy disturbed Oppenheimer and his attorneys. Already they had been contacted by a writer for the *New York Times*, James Reston, who was aware of the charges and was about to publish a story on the hearing against Oppenheimer.

At Garrison's request, though, Reston had delayed breaking the story. But when Garrison phoned Reston that day, Reston said he couldn't wait any longer. Garrison authorized him to go ahead, and by the next day the story had been picked up by newspapers and radio stations across the country: One of the nation's most famous scientists had been suspended by the Atomic Energy Commission and was forced to defend himself against charges that he had ties to Communists.

The next morning at the hearing, these newspaper articles were the first item on the agenda. Chairman Gray was irritated with Oppenheimer and his attorneys, particularly since it was clear that many documents from the case had been released to Reston without Gray's knowledge.

Gray's anger influenced the way he handled the witnesses appearing for Oppenheimer. He told Oppenheimer's attorney that witnesses would be heard at times suited "to the convenience of this board and not the convenience of the witnesses."[2]

One major difference between the hearing and the way a trial would be handled was that Oppenheimer, who was the "accused," took the stand at the beginning of the proceedings to tell his story. Frequently, though, Oppenheimer's testimony was interrupted so that other witnesses could speak for him.

For almost three days, as his attorney questioned him, Oppenheimer talked about his work for the government and his personal life, including his brother, Frank, and Frank's membership in the Communist Party.

In the middle of the third day, Roger Robb, the attorney

for the Atomic Energy Commission, took over and began a cross-examination that would last for twelve hours over three days. Time and again Robb showed himself a powerful foe, a skillful attorney who far outshone the attorneys defending Oppenheimer. Robb would build traps with his questions and then lead Oppenheimer into them. Robb would induce Oppenheimer to make a strong statement on a subject. Then Robb would surprise Oppenheimer with contradictory statements taken from interviews that Oppenheimer had had with security officers during World War II.

At one point Robb asked Oppenheimer about a letter he wrote in 1943 to try to get the Army to assign Private Giovanni Rossi Lomanitz, his former student, to the Radiation Laboratory at Berkeley.

Robb asked Oppenheimer: "Of course, you would not have written that letter if you had known Lomanitz was a Communist, would you?"

Oppenheimer answered flatly, "No."[3]

But later Robb pointed out that three weeks before Oppenheimer wrote the letter about Lomanitz he had told security officers that he knew that Lomanitz was a Communist Party member.

Of course, Oppenheimer was answering questions based on ten-year-old memories, while Robb had access to transcripts of the interviews with security officers. But the board was left wondering: Was Oppenheimer merely forgetful? Had he altered the facts in his own mind, as all human beings do to some extent, in order to rationalize his own failings? Or was he intentionally trying to lie and cover up?

During the first day of cross-examination Robb took up one of the most sensitive issues of all, Oppenheimer's interview with security officers about the conversation with Haakon Chevalier that had taken place in his kitchen during World War II.

On the sidelines Lloyd Garrison watched as Robb wore down Oppenheimer bit by bit and wondered why Oppenheimer made no attempt to pause or rephrase his answers in a framework that would shield him.

Robb: "Now let us go back to your interview with Colonel Pash. Did you tell Pash the truth about this thing?"

Oppenheimer: "No."

Robb: "You lied to him?"

Oppenheimer: "Yes."

Robb: "Didn't you say that X [Chevalier] had approached three people?"

Oppenheimer: "Probably."

Robb: "Why did you do that, Doctor?"

Oppenheimer: "Because I was an idiot."

Robb later recalled that moment as the turning point of the hearing and said: "I remember him sitting there with his hands between his knees, wringing his hands between his knees, head bowed, white as a sheet. I felt sick."

Robb went home that night and told his wife, "I've just seen a man destroy himself."[4]

But that wasn't the end of Oppenheimer's agony. As the final blow, Robb asked, "Isn't it a fair statement today, Dr. Oppenheimer, that according to your testimony now you told not one lie to Colonel Pash, but a whole fabrication and tissue of lies?"

Oppenheimer's reply: "Right."

Garrison would later regret that at that moment he didn't raise an objection. "It lies heavy on my conscience," he told the board five days later, "that I did not at that time object to the impression that was trying to be conveyed to this board of a whole series of lies when in fact there was one story which was told."[5]

His objection was too little and too late. The damage had been done.

Many have speculated about why Oppenheimer answered as he did without more explanation of his past actions. After he chose to take on the ordeal of the hearing, why surrender so readily without explanation? Did he enjoy the role of martyr? Was his weakness as a witness a remnant of the self-destructiveness that had troubled him during his college years? Was he trying to punish himself for what happened to Chevalier, who had problems for years in trying to find a job because of Oppenheimer's statements to Colonel Pash?

By Friday, Robb had begun to probe Oppenheimer's actions and opinions about the H-bomb. He asked for details of the October 1949 meeting of the General Advisory Committee where everyone present had voted unanimously against continued research on the super.

Did everyone on the committee give his opinion on the bomb? Robb asked. Yes, Oppenheimer said, except for Glenn Seaborg who was absent, in Sweden.

Robb: "You didn't know either how he felt about it. He was just not there."

Oppenheimer: "He was in Sweden and there was no communication with him. . . ."

Robb: "You didn't poll him by mail or anything?"

Oppenheimer: "This was not a convenient thing to do."

Very quickly, Robb produced the letter from Seaborg dated October 14, 1949, and Oppenheimer, stumbling, replied: "I am going to say before I see that that I had no recollection of it."

Oppenheimer tried to defend himself by pointing out that at future meetings Seaborg had chances to give his views on the H-bomb but did not do so. But Robb pulled out other evidence in an effort to make it look as if Oppenheimer had been lying rather than forgetful.

He reminded Oppenheimer that in January 1950 he had failed to mention Seaborg's letter while testifying about the H-bomb to the Joint Atomic Energy Committee of Congress.

Oppenheimer and his attorneys at that point demanded to see the transcript of the meeting before the Joint Atomic Energy Committee. What had the committee asked Oppenheimer, and what specifically had he replied? But the hearing board refused to let the attorneys see the material. The necessity of maintaining government secrecy would not allow the board to release the transcript.

Over the weekend, at the home of a friend in Washington, Oppenheimer and his attorneys sat down to discuss the case with Joseph Volpe, the former general counsel to the Atomic Energy Commission.

Volpe was outraged by what he heard was happening at the hearings. He had drawn up the procedures for such hearings while serving with the commission and had never intended these sessions to turn into adversary proceedings. "After an hour or so, I finally said, 'Robert, tell them to shove it, leave it, don't go on with it because I don't think you can win.' "[6] But Oppenheimer and his advisers were determined to press on in spite of this warning.

Once Oppenheimer left the witness chair, more of his defense witnesses appeared. But just like Oppenheimer, many found their testimony distorted by Roger Robb. General Groves, now a businessman working for the Remington Rand Corporation, appeared and said he would be "amazed" if Oppenheimer had ever committed a disloyal act. He also said that he felt that Oppenheimer's initial refusal to tell him Haakon Chevalier's name was "the typical American school boy attitude that there is something wicked about telling on a friend."[7]

But Robb cast doubt on some of Groves's testimony by getting him to admit that Oppenheimer could not be cleared for security purposes under the new, stricter standards adopted after the end of World War II.

Over the next several days a long line of notable scientists testified about the character and loyalty of Robert Oppenheimer. Among them were the Nobel Prize winners Enrico

Fermi, Isidor Rabi, and Hans Bethe and major government figures such as James Conant, David Lilienthal, and Vannevar Bush.

In many cases Robb compromised the testimony of Oppenheimer's witnesses. One witness, who said he would trust Oppenheimer as he would his own son, admitted he had not known that Frank Oppenheimer was ever a Communist. Another respected scientist from Los Alamos was trapped into conceding that he had hired a suspected Communist.

One of the most effective witnesses for Oppenheimer was Isidor I. Rabi, who had been in on the General Advisory Committee's discussion of the H-bomb. Rabi outlined the complex tangle of issues involved in developing a new super bomb: whether the development of an H-bomb would interfere with providing nuclear material to build additional fission bombs; whether a fusion, or super bomb, could be made small enough to allow it to be delivered by an airplane; and what the program to develop an H-bomb would cost.

"We didn't even know whether this thing contradicted the laws of physics," Rabi said.[8] In fact, he pointed out, the kind of super that was being discussed before the General Advisory Committee was never even built. Rabi also argued that Oppenheimer's encounter with Haakon Chevalier should be viewed in the context of history. In 1943 when it occurred, he said, Russia was our World War II ally. In 1954 the Soviet Union was our enemy in a cold war. No single incident in Oppenheimer's life should be divorced from his entire life.

The charges against Oppenheimer, Rabi said, "didn't seem to me the sort of thing that called for this kind of proceeding . . . against a man who has accomplished what Dr. Oppenheimer has accomplished." Rabi went on: "We have the A-bomb and a whole series of [them] . . . what more do you want, mermaids? This is just a tremendous achievement. If the end of that road is this kind of hearing, which can't help but be humiliating, I [think it is] a pretty bad show."[9]

Vannevar Bush, then president of the Carnegie Institution in Washington, told the board it was making a serious mistake in its probe of Oppenheimer, who was in trouble merely because he disagreed with other government officials. "Here is a man who is being pilloried because he had strong opinions and had the temerity to express them," he said. "If this country ever gets to the point where we come that near to the Russian system, we are certainly not in any condition to attempt to lead the free world toward the benefits of democracy."[10]

This criticism from a respected scientist who had served in a number of federal positions shocked the board. In fact, Chairman Gray privately sought out Robb to ask if there was any way to bring the hearing to a close, but Robb told him that there was not.[11]

Then, on April 27 the government began to present its case against Oppenheimer. Never before in any previous Atomic Energy Commission security hearing had government officials felt compelled to do this.

Among the first witnesses was Kenneth Pitzer, director of research for the Atomic Energy Commission, who charged that Oppenheimer's lack of enthusiasm had affected recruiting for the super.

Ernest Lawrence had planned to testify against Oppenheimer, but associates at Berkeley persuaded him not to. In addition, Lawrence became ill; this gave him an additional excuse not to appear. Lawrence also tried to persuade Luis Alvarez, a fellow professor of physics at Berkeley, not to testify. "He [Lawrence] said people had convinced him that the Radiation Laboratory would be greatly harmed if he testified and that he [and several other scientists] and I were viewed as a cabal bent on destroying Robert," Alvarez later said.[12]

Alvarez canceled his plans to testify, but that night Lewis Strauss, chairman of the Atomic Energy Commission, called him and urged that he appear. "As a parting shot he prophesied that if I didn't come to Washington the next day I wouldn't be able to look myself in the mirror for the rest of my life," Alvarez said.[13]

Alvarez was convinced and flew to Washington, where he talked for nearly a whole day about his difficulties in 1949 in promoting the H-bomb project. One of the board members, Ward Evans, then asked what Alvarez thought Oppenheimer's opposition to the H-bomb meant.

"By itself it means absolutely nothing because I have many other friends in the scientific world who feel precisely this way," Alvarez said. "The point I was trying to bring out was that every time I have found a person who felt this way, I have seen Dr. Oppenheimer's influence on that person's mind."

"It doesn't mean that he was disloyal?" Evans asked.

"Absolutely not, sir," Alvarez replied, but he later qualified his statement by saying that Oppenheimer had shown "exceedingly poor judgment."[14]

While the government presented its case, Oppenheimer had the chance to confront his first accuser, William Borden, the man who had written the letter to the FBI that had touched off the Atomic Energy Commission investigation and hearing. This confrontation seemed as if it might have the potential for greatly damaging Oppenheimer's case. Would Borden present new evidence that might shock and persuade the board? It didn't turn out that way.

After Borden's letter was reread to the board, which also had copies of it, the board dismissed Borden's central conclusion that Oppenheimer was an agent linked to the Soviet Union. Chairman Gray said there was "no evidence" to support the claim that Oppenheimer had volunteered to comply with any request for information.

After thinking about the matter over a weekend, Oppenheimer's lawyers decided not to cross-examine Borden. It was apparent that the board thought little of his charges, and yet those charges were the cause of the hearing in the first place.

Instead it was another witness, a fellow scientist, Edward Teller, who gave the most damaging testimony against Oppenheimer.

Despite his differences with Oppenheimer, which had grown bitter during the years that he was pursuing funding for the H-bomb, Teller was ambivalent about the hearing. "I was convinced then and continue to believe now that the hearing should never have occurred," Teller said years later.

So then why did he appear against Oppenheimer? Some have suggested that it was because of loyalty to Strauss, who had supported Teller in the past and could be of greater help in the future. According to Teller, before he appeared at the hearing, he met with attorney Roger Robb, and Robb asked him how he would testify—for or against Oppenheimer's clearance. "I had no difficulty with my reply," Teller said, "I would testify for Oppie's clearance."[15]

Robb then read Teller a section of Oppenheimer's testimony about the Chevalier affair. "I will never forget the shock that this portion of the testimony produced in me," Teller said. "Robb asked me again, 'Should Oppenheimer be cleared?' I could only tell him that I did not know."[16]

Later Robb asked Teller similar questions at the hearing. Did he think Oppenheimer was disloyal to the United States? Teller replied, "I have always assumed, and I now assume, that he is loyal to the United States."

Robb went further: "Do you or do you not believe that Dr. Oppenheimer is a security risk?"

Teller: "In a great number of instances, I have seen Dr. Oppenheimer act—I understood that Dr. Oppenheimer acted—in a way which for me was exceedingly hard to understand, and his actions frankly appeared to me confused and complicated. To this extent I feel I would like to see the vital interests of this country in hands which I understand better and therefore trust more. In this very limited sense I would like to express a feeling that I would feel personally more secure if public matters would rest in other hands."[17]

This was the first serious damage that Teller dealt to Oppenheimer, but there was more to come. After his testimony ended, Chairman Gray took up the questioning.

Gray: "Do you feel it would endanger the common defense and security to grant clearance to Dr. Oppenheimer?"

Teller: "I believe that Dr. Oppenheimer's character is such that he would not knowingly and willingly do anything that is designed to endanger the safety of this country. To the extent, therefore, that your question is directed toward intent, I would say I do not see any reason to deny clearance."[18]

But Teller did not stop there; instead he went on to deliver a more destructive blow: "If it is a question of wisdom and judgment, as demonstrated by actions since 1945, then I would say one would be wiser not to grant clearance."

These remarks would not only damage Oppenheimer, of course, they would upset and outrage the entire scientific community, which had begun to see Oppenheimer as a martyr regardless of his opinions.

After testifying, Teller rose from his chair and turned to Oppenheimer, who was seated on the sofa behind him, and offered his hand. As they shook hands, Teller said, "I'm sorry."

Oppenheimer replied in a polite tone, edged with irony: "After what you've just said, I don't know what you mean."

After several more witnesses and rebuttal testimony by Oppenheimer, Garrison gave his summation to the board. Although some lawyers would later criticize him for not being more aggressive during the hearing, most agree that his final statement was excellent. He managed to deliver a polished oration that summarized more than three thousand pages of testimony.

Finally on May 6, 1954, after proceedings that had lasted longer than most criminal trials, the hearing in the matter of J. Robert Oppenheimer came to an end.

17

"I had very little sense of self"

After a trial must come the verdict. But members of the hearing board first went home to collect their thoughts and rest for ten days.

On May 17 they returned to Washington. Two of them, Gordon Gray and Thomas Morgan, found that they had reached similar conclusions, negative to Oppenheimer. But Ward Evans, they were shocked to find, disagreed with them, despite the fact that he had once revealed anti-Oppenheimer views. They were sure that fellow scientists must have influenced his vote, but Evans denied it.

For ten days they worked on their respective reports on the twenty-four charges, which they divided into two categories: the single charge concerning the H-bomb and the twenty-three involving Oppenheimer's prewar leftist connections.

Although all three board members found that many of the charges involving Oppenheimer's leftist connections were true, they also said, "We have come to a clear conclusion, which should be reassuring to the people of this country, that he is a loyal citizen."[1]

All three also agreed that none of the evidence supported the contention that Oppenheimer had opposed the super, or H-bomb, because of some attachment to the Soviet Union. But Gray and Morgan did conclude that even though Oppenheimer had not openly opposed the H-bomb, "enthusiastic support on his part would perhaps have encouraged other leading scientists to work on the program" and "the opposition to the H-bomb by many persons connected with the atomic energy program, of which Dr. Oppenheimer was the most experienced, most powerful and most effective member, did delay the initiation of concerted effort which led to the development of a thermonuclear weapon."[2] In other words, Oppenheimer was being condemned for not being enthusiastic enough about the H-bomb.

The two also found that Oppenheimer had been discreet in the past about handling government secrets but criticized Oppenheimer's friendship with Haakon Chevalier because of Chevalier's background. Finally, Gray and Morgan concluded that Oppenheimer's security clearance should not be reinstated.

Among their conclusions were the following:

"We find that Dr. Oppenheimer's continuing conduct and associations have reflected a serious disregard for the requirements of the security system.

"We find his conduct in the hydrogen-bomb program sufficiently disturbing as to raise a doubt as to whether his future participation, if characterized by the same attitudes in a government program relating to the national defense, would be clearly consistent with the best interests of security."

Evans had also put together a minority report, which the other board members read but found poorly written. Surprisingly, Roger Robb helped him rewrite it. As Robb later said, if Evans's report had looked too disorganized, "it would look as though we put a nincompoop on the board."[3]

Evans began by saying that Oppenheimer's clearance should be reinstated. He noted that back in 1947, when the Atomic Energy Commission had first cleared the scientist, it had had most of the information that the hearing board had. "They apparently were aware of his associations and his left-wing policies; yet they cleared him," Evans said. "They took a chance on him because of his special talents and he continued to do a good job."[4]

Oppenheimer did not hinder development of the H-bomb, Evans said; "If his opposition to the H-bomb caused any people not to work on it, it was because of his intellectual prominence and influence over scientific people, and not because of any subversive tendencies."[5]

If Oppenheimer's clearance was not restored, Evans said, it "will be a black mark on the escutcheon of our country."[6]

The two reports traveled next to the Atomic Energy Commission's general manager, Kenneth D. Nichols, who soon sent a letter to Oppenheimer advising him of the outcome. Nichols himself began composing his own recommendation to the five Atomic Energy Commission members who would make the final decision on Oppenheimer's security clearance.

Oppenheimer and his attorneys were distressed and were particularly worried that the verdict might be made public without any rebuttal. So Garrison drafted a reply to the board's opinion and released the verdict and his letter to the press. Throughout early June a war waged in the newspapers over charges and countercharges from the Oppenheimer side and the Atomic Energy Commission. On June 15 the Atomic Energy Commission even released a transcript of the hearing.

At about the same time Nichols released his own recommendation, which was even more harsh than the findings of the hearing board. Although he admitted that there was no direct evidence that Oppenheimer had ever given away a secret or was disloyal, Nichols said the record showed that Oppenheimer had been "a Communist in every respect except for the fact that he did not carry a party card." Oppenheimer had been "deeply and consciously involved"[7] with hardened and militant Communists at a time when he was a man of mature judgment, Nichols said.

In discussing the Chevalier incident, Nichols was equally as critical. Why did Oppenheimer invent a complicated story to "show that Chevalier was not innocent, but on the contrary was deeply involved in an espionage conspiracy?" Nichols asked.[8]

"His own testimony shows that he was guilty of deliberate misrepresentations and falsifications either in his interview with Colonel Pash or in his testimony before the board; and such misrepresentation and falsifications constituted criminal . . . dishonest . . . conduct."[9]

Nichols's ruling was secretly forwarded to the Atomic Energy Commission, headed by Lewis Strauss, without a word to Garrison or Oppenheimer. Some had thought that the commission might provide some hope for Oppenheimer since three of its members were Democrats, appointed by Truman, and only two were Republicans. But as it turned out, only one commissioner, Henry DeWolf Smyth, a physics professor at Princeton, sympathized with Oppenheimer.

In some ways Smyth's vote for Oppenheimer was strange in that in the ten years he had known Oppenheimer he had found the scientist arrogant and unlikable. At one point he told some assistants who helped him in writing his minority report, ". . . it's funny I should be going to all this trouble for Oppenheimer. I don't even like the guy much."[10]

In the end the four other board members voted against Oppenheimer because of his past associations with Communists, including Chevalier, and because of what Strauss termed Oppenheimer's "defects of character."[11]

However, Smyth's minority report noted that there was no indication that Oppenheimer had ever given away any secrets. "The past 15 years of his life have been investigated and reinvestigated," he said. "For much of the last 11 years, he has been under actual surveillance, his movements watched, his conversations noted, his mail and telephone calls checked."[12]

At 4 P.M. on June 29 the commissioners' opinions were handed to the press, and Oppenheimer's battle was over. Oppenheimer and his attorneys had already decided not to try to take his fight to the courts. They briefly considered appealing to the president but then gave up the idea. It was unlikely Eisenhower would overrule the board, and he might possibly side with the verdict, adding further weight to the charges.

Was there something that Oppenheimer could have done to prevent this painful ordeal? Did he play into the hands of his enemies, and why? Some, such as Edward Teller, believed that Oppenheimer had been engaged in a battle with no purpose, that he had entered it purely out of his concept of himself as a martyr.

Time magazine, in an article written after the transcript of the hearing became public, commented that "in the list of witnesses against J. Robert Oppenheimer, the most effective was J. Robert Oppenheimer himself."[13]

Even Oppenheimer's good friend, Isidor Rabi, felt that Oppenheimer could have prevented his destruction. "If I'd been in on it [the hearing], maybe I could have gotten him to manage the case in the way I thought. I would simply have advised him to stand up and say, 'This is what I accomplished for the United States. There is a record. I see no reason for a retrial. If you find it in your hearts to do this, there it is. I hope you have a long life and live to regret it. I will have no part of it.' Period. And walk out. Instead he stood up there and spilled his guts."[14] How could Oppenheimer have performed so effectively before the House Un-American Activities Committee just a few years before and then go on to stumble in this Atomic Energy Commission hearing?

Later in life Oppenheimer said that he thought he had not been careful enough in answering questions, that he had answered too quickly, "the way a soldier does in combat, I suppose. So much is happening or may be about to happen that there is no time to be aware of anything except the next move. . . . Like someone in a fight—and this was a fight—I had very little sense of self."[15]

Identity was a problem for Oppenheimer, Rabi agrees. Oppenheimer was never completely sure of who he was. "He never got to be an integrated personality. It happens some times, with many people, but more frequently, perhaps, because of their situation, with brilliant Jewish people. With enormous capacities in every direction, it is hard to choose. He wanted everything."[16]

As news of the verdict spread, there were repercussions on all sides. President Eisenhower declined to comment on the case. At Princeton, Albert Einstein and other colleagues of Oppenheimer's publicly announced their support for him. Most newspapers were favorable to the verdict, but the *Washington Post* asked: "Will the security of the country really be stronger because Dr. Oppenheimer has been excluded from the program to which he has contributed so much?"[17]

Many scientists who had disagreed with Oppenheimer about his support of legislation that they found objectionable now rushed to his defense.

In mid-July Oppenheimer and his family set off for a holiday in the Virgin Islands while rumors and news reports still swirled about them. When they flew back to New York in late August, a team of FBI agents was waiting for him, and they interrogated him at the airport about a newspaper column that had claimed that a scientist vacationing in the Virgin Islands had been approached by the Russians. Oppenheimer denied the report, but as he drove home, a team of FBI agents trailed him.

18

*"The government never had
a servant more devoted"*

Many said that Oppenheimer seemed to age visibly after the hearing. His gaunt figure grew more haggard; the lines in his face seemed to be etched more deeply.

When asked by a writer, John Mason Brown, if the hearing had been like a dry crucifixion, Oppenheimer replied, "You know, it wasn't so very dry. I can still feel the warm blood on my hands."[1]

Nor did the pain end after the hearing. His onetime friend Haakon Chevalier finally learned from newspaper accounts about Oppenheimer's conversations with security officials about him. That was why, Chevalier concluded, his career had been stymied at every turn. He wrote bitter letters to Oppenheimer and then books detailing their friendship and Oppenheimer's betrayal.

At first it looked as if Oppenheimer's career at Princeton might be jeopardized. The chairman of the board of trustees of the Institute for Advanced Study decided to call a meeting to discuss whether Oppenheimer should be asked to resign.

But by the time the meeting was held in October, the furor over Oppenheimer's hearing had begun to subside, and he was reelected as director of the Institute. Even Lewis Strauss, who served on the Institute board, had voted for Oppenheimer.

At the Institute, Oppenheimer continued to build a warm atmosphere for physicists and philosophers as well. Among the famous names who visited the Institute were P. A. M. Dirac, Niels Bohr, Wolfgang Pauli, Hans Bethe, R. D. Lee, and C. N. Yang. Lee and Yang had made great advances in the field of elementary particle physics and won the Nobel Prize for their work in 1957.

Oppenheimer's way of life continued to be one of elegance. "Certainly by physicists' standards," said one fellow at the Institute, "Oppenheimer was a wealthy man, and he knew how to enjoy his money."[2]

But the hearing and its painful conclusion had taken its toll on Oppenheimer and his family. Some referred to the Oppenheimer home as "Bourbon Manor" because both Kitty and Robert Oppenheimer were known for their heavy drinking. Kitty developed a diseased pancreas, which required heavy drug treatments.

Oppenheimer remained awkward with his children, and in Peter's teenage years he and his son developed differences, particularly surrounding Peter's grades in school. In 1958, when Peter failed to get into Princeton, Oppenheimer left his son at home in summer school while he took Kitty and Toni on a European lecture tour.

For some years Robert Oppenheimer did manage to stay out of the news. However, when Russia launched its sputnik satellite, outdoing the United States in space research, the drive was on to upgrade science and research across the nation. Many called for Oppenheimer to be reinstated. Wernher von Braun, the German refugee who had worked for Hitler on rocket research and then came to the United States to work on the space program, told Congress that the Oppenheimer affair had "hurt the whole scientific community very badly."[3] Some officials attempted to arrange the restoration of Oppenheimer's security clearance, but little came of the matter.

Although Oppenheimer no longer had an official post in the United States, the International Atomic Energy Agency chose him to serve on a multination conference on high-energy physics in 1960. The next year the Organization of American States invited him to make a lecture tour in Latin America.

After John F. Kennedy became president, the push was on to heal Oppenheimer's wounds, to restore the cloak of honor that had been torn away in the security hearing. To the liberal intellectuals in Kennedy's Cabinet, what Oppenheimer had done had been heroic.

First, Glenn Seaborg, now chairman of the Atomic Energy Commission, asked Oppenheimer if he would like a new security hearing that would restore his clearance. "Not on your life," Oppenheimer told him.[4]

Next, Oppenheimer's supporters decided that Oppenheimer was a good candidate for the Fermi Award, given annually by the Atomic Energy Commission in the name of Enrico Fermi, who had died of cancer in the 1950s. Usually, the commission asked a number of prominent scientists for their nominations. Among those in 1963 who voted for Oppenheimer was Edward Teller, who was anxious to end his differences with Oppenheimer. Oppenheimer's nomination was approved unanimously by the General Advisory Committee of the commission and by the commission itself. President Kennedy announced that he would present the award himself in November. But before that could take place, Kennedy was assassinated.

The presentation was eventually made by the new president, Lyndon Johnson, on December 2, 1963. While Oppenheimer's friends and family members watched, Johnson gave Oppenheimer the citation, a medal, and a check for fifty thousand dollars. In response Oppenheimer said, "I think it is just possible, Mr. President, that it has taken some charity and some courage for you to make this award today. That would seem to me a good augury for all our futures."[5]

Edward Teller, the recipient of the award in 1962, attended the ceremony and shook Oppenheimer's hand at a reception afterward. The two never became friends again, but at least this was a token of a truce between them.

The next year there was another sentimental gesture of reconciliation: Oppenheimer was invited to return to Los Alamos to give a memorial speech about Niels Bohr, the physicist, who had died in 1962. The audience jammed into the auditorium and gave Oppenheimer a standing ovation. The same year Oppenheimer had another homecoming at the University of California at Berkeley, where an audience of 12,500 heard him speak.

But the clock was ticking toward the end for Oppenheimer. He had wasted away to a frail shadow, and in 1965 he had to give up his post as director of the Institute to become senior professor of theoretical physics. In 1966 he was diagnosed with throat cancer and had to give up his professorship as well. He finally quit smoking and began to suck throat lozenges to ease the pain in his throat. In June he managed to attend the Princeton graduation with the help of a cane and leg brace so that he could receive an honorary degree.

In one of his final interviews with a reporter he was asked to comment about how his life had turned out. Oppenheimer told an anecdote about a general who was reviewing his troops after a battle. When the officer stopped to ask one soldier about his role in the conflict, "the soldier," said Oppenheimer, "replied, 'I survived.' "[6]

On a Saturday night, February 18, 1967, at Olden Manor at Princeton, Oppenheimer died at age sixty-two. A week later his friends and family gathered at Princeton's Alexander Hall to pay their final respects to him.

The hall was packed with the nation's brightest scientists and top officials, those who had shared experiences with him at Los Alamos and who had known him in academia and in government: Isidor Rabi, Robert Serber, retired General Leslie Groves, and David Lilienthal.

George Kennan, a colleague of Oppenheimer's at Princeton and a state department official, was among those who spoke that day. "On no one," he said, "did there ever rest with greater cruelty the dilemmas evoked by the recent conquest by human beings of a power over nature out of all proportion to their moral strength."

In the midst of all of his problems with the government, Kennan said, Oppenheimer remained passionately loyal to his country.

"The truth is," Kennan said, "that the U.S. government never had a servant more devoted at heart than this one, in the sense of wanting to make a constructive contribution; and I know of nothing more tragic than the series of mistakes (in part, no doubt, his own, but in what small part) that made it impossible for him to render this contribution—that obliged him to spend the last decade and a half of his life eating out his heart in frustration over the consciousness that the talents he knew himself to possess, once welcomed and used by the official establishment of his country to develop the destructive possibilities of nuclear science, were rejected when it came to the development of the great positive ones he believed that science to possess . . ."[7]

19

"We are not only scientists; we are men, too"

In part, what befell Oppenheimer was the result of his own mistakes: his pride and capacity to wound others whom he considered less intelligent than himself, his betrayal of friends, his own naive associations with Communists, the self-destructive impulse that led him to continue the security hearing despite the disastrous turn it had taken.

But the security hearing he went through was a travesty, a betrayal of the protections that the Bill of Rights normally gives to U.S. citizens. Oppenheimer was forced to undergo a shadow trial, one in which he was certain to be convicted before the jury even heard him speak.

Although late in his life there were attempts to mend fences and repair the damage done to him psychologically and professionally, his security clearance was never restored. During the years that he was shut out of political and public life, the nation lost his advice on many issues involving nuclear physics.

Furthermore, his security "trial" not only shattered his life, it shattered others as well and created a great gulf among scientists in this country and animosity among many in the scientific establishment and the government.

For years after the hearing many scientists blamed Edward Teller for what had happened to Oppenheimer. Even as late as 1982, when the surviving Los Alamos scientists held a reunion to mark the fortieth anniversary of the year they began work on the atomic bomb, a physicist at the party told a writer that "Teller put the knife in Robert's back and twisted it."[1]

Teller himself said a year earlier: "What happened over the Oppenheimer case not only polarized the scientific community but also brought about the situation that at least ninety percent of the scientists and probably more consider it immoral to cooperate in any way with the military. Our present military weakness goes back to those days."[2]

But at the same time Oppenheimer's career and fall from grace made the nation's scientists more aware than ever that they could no longer shield themselves from the outside world in their laboratories; that they could no longer produce technological breakthroughs such as the atomic bomb without taking some responsibility for how they would be used. Since Oppenheimer's death many scientists have turned statesmen as well, eager to have an influence over how the nation uses the fruits of scientific research.

Oppenheimer was among the first to recognize the connection, to realize that the ivory tower of science had fallen forever. As he said in his speech at Los Alamos in 1945: "We are not only scientists; we are men, too."

After his death Oppenheimer's wife, Kitty, lived only a few more years. She became ill in 1972 while on a vacation in the Virgin Islands and died a short time later.

Toni Oppenheimer married and divorced and in 1977 killed herself after an unhappy romance. Her brother, Peter, still lives with his family in the mountains of New Mexico that his father had loved so much.

Notes

CHAPTER 1

1. Peter Goodchild, *J. Robert Oppenheimer: Shatterer of Worlds* (New York: Fromm International, reprint, 1985), 11.
2. *Robert Oppenheimer: Letters and Recollections*, ed. Alice Kimball Smith and Charles Weiner (Cambridge: Mass.: Harvard University Press, 1980), 1.
3. J. Robert Oppenheimer, interview with Thomas S. Kuhn on November 18, 1963, on file with the Archive for History of Quantum Physics, available at the University of California, Berkeley, and the American Institute of Physics, New York, 1.
4. *Robert Oppenheimer: Letters and Recollections*, 4.
5. Goodchild, *J. Robert Oppenheimer*, 12.
6. Oppenheimer interview with Kuhn, 2.
7. Ibid., 3
8. *Robert Oppenheimer: Letters and Recollections*, 6.
9. Goodchild, *J. Robert Oppenheimer*, 12.

CHAPTER 2

1. Oppenheimer interview with Kuhn, 3.
2. *Robert Oppenheimer: Letters and Recollections*, 18–19.
3. Ibid., 61.
4. Oppenheimer interview with Kuhn, 8.
5. *Robert Oppenheimer: Letters and Recollections*, 87.

6. Ibid., 88–89.
7. Ibid., 92.
8. Oppenheimer interview with Kuhn, 21.
9. Robert Jungk, *Brighter Than a Thousand Suns* (New York: Harcourt, Brace and Co., 1958), 23.
10. Oppenheimer interview with Kuhn, 18.

CHAPTER 3

1. *Robert Oppenheimer: Letters and Recollections*, 132.
2. Abraham Pais, Isidor Rabi, Glenn Seaborg, Robert Serber, and Victor Weisskopf, *Oppenheimer* (New York: Charles Scribner's Sons, 1969), 48.
3. Glenn Seaborg, interview with author March, 17, 1987.
4. Pais et al., *Oppenheimer*, 7.
5. Goodchild, *J. Robert Oppenheimer*, 30.
6. U.S. Atomic Energy Commission, *In the Matter of J. Robert Oppenheimer: Transcript of Hearing before Personnel Security Board, Washington, D.C.* (U.S. Government Printing Office, Washington, D.C., 1954), 8.
7. Ibid., 8, 9.
8. Goodchild, *J. Robert Oppenheimer*, 39.

CHAPTER 4

1. Jungk, *Brighter Than a Thousand Suns*, 48.
2. Ibid., 79.
3. Goodchild, *J. Robert Oppenheimer*, 48.
4. Ibid., 51
5. Information supplied by Edward Teller in response to author's request for interview.

CHAPTER 5

1. Leslie R. Groves, *Now It Can Be Told* (New York: Harper & Row, 1962), 63.
2. Goodchild, *J. Robert Oppenheimer*, 66.
3. Groves, *Now It Can Be Told*, 63.

CHAPTER 6

1. *In the Matter of J. Robert Oppenheimber: Transcript of Hearing*, 13.
2. Norris Bradbury, interview with author, February 26, 1987.
3. Isidor I. Rabi, interview with author, March 3, 1987.
4. Hans Bethe, interview with author, March 5, 1987.
5. Information supplied by Edward Teller.

6. *Robert Oppenheimer: Letters and Recollections*, 264.
7. Stanley A. Blumberg and Gwinn Owens, *Energy and Conflict: The Life and Times of Edward Teller* (New York: G. P. Putnam's Sons, 1976), 130.

CHAPTER 7

1. Goodchild, *J. Robert Oppenheimer*, 93.

CHAPTER 8

1. *Robert Oppenheimer: Letters and Recollections*, 286.
2. Richard G. Hewlett and Oscar E. Anderson Jr., *The new world 1939– 1946: Vol. 1 of a History of the United States Atomic Energy Commission 1939–1946* (University Park, Pa.: The Pennsylvania State University Press, 1962), 1:248.
3. Goodchild, *J. Robert Oppenheimer*, 116.
4. *Robert Oppenheimer: Letters and Recollections*, 288.

CHAPTER 9

1. Groves, *Now It Can Be Told*, 264.
2. Richard Rhodes, *The Making of the Atomic Bomb* (New York: Simon and Schuster, 1986), 647.
3. *In the Matter of J. Robert Oppenheimer: Transcript of Hearing*, 236.
4. Interview with Isidor I. Rabi.
5. Jungk, *Brighter Than a Thousand Suns*, 185.
6. Information supplied by Edward Teller.
7. Ibid.
8. Ibid.
9. *Robert Oppenheimer: Letters and Recollections*, 317.
10. Ibid., 290.
11. Lansing Lamont, *Day of Trinity* (New York: Atheneum, 1965), 164.
12. Goodchild, *J. Robert Oppenheimer*, 152–153.
13. Ibid., 155.

CHAPTER 10

1. Rhodes, *The Making of the Atomic Bomb*, 663.
2. Lamont, *Day of Trinity*, 212.
3. Rhodes, *The Making of the Atomic Bomb*, 668.
4. Lamont, *Day of Trinity*, 226.
5. Ibid., 231.
6. William L. Laurence, *Men and Atoms* (New York: Simon and Schuster, 1959), 117.

7. Lamont, *Day of Trinity*, 240.
8. Jungk, *Brighter Than a Thousand Suns*, 201.
9. Groves, *Now It Can Be Told*, 438.
10. Goodchild, *J. Robert Oppenheimer*, 162.
11. Lamont, *Day of Trinity*, 242.
12. Ibid., 243.
13. Ibid., 254.
14. Stephane Groueff, *Manhattan Project: The Untold Story of the Making of the Atomic Bomb* (New York: Bantam Books, reprint, 1968), 410.
15. Lamont, *Day of Trinity*, 242.

CHAPTER 11

1. Rhodes, *The Making of the Atomic Bomb*, 693.
2. John Hersey, *Hiroshima* (New York: Bantam Books, 1959), 33, 34.
3. Ibid., 61.
4. Rhodes, *The Making of the Atomic Bomb*, 734.
5. Ibid.
6. Jungk, *Brighter Than a Thousand Suns*, 221.
7. *Robert Oppenheimer: Letters and Recollections*, 292.
8. Groves, *Now It Can Be Told*, 352.
9. Laura Fermi, *Atoms in the Family* (Chicago: University of Chicago Press, 1954), 240.
10. Lamont, *Day of Trinity*, 267.
11. *Robert Oppenheimer: Letters and Recollections*, 294.
12. Ibid., 297.
13. Rhodes, *The Making of the Atomic Bomb*, 758.

CHAPTER 12

1. *Robert Oppenheimer: Letters and Recollections*, 315–323.
2. *In the Matter of J. Robert Oppenheimer: Transcript of Hearing*, 15.
3. Ibid., 16.
4. Hewlett and Anderson, *The New World*, 432.
5. Ibid., 445.
6. Goodchild, *J. Robert Oppenheimer*, 180.
7. Ibid., 180.
8. Ibid., 182.
9. Pais et al. *Oppenheimer*, 50.
10. Ibid., 51.

CHAPTER 13

1. David E. Lilienthal, *The Journals of David E. Lilienthal* (New York: Harper & Row, 1966), 2:456.

2. Goodchild, *J. Robert Oppenheimer*, 188.
3. Ibid., 191.
4. Ibid., 195.

CHAPTER 14

1. Information supplied by Edward Teller.
2. Goodchild, *J. Robert Oppenheimer*, 196.
3. Ibid., 197.
4. *In the Matter of J. Robert Oppenheimer: Transcript of Hearing*, 714.
5. Luis W. Alvarez, *Alvarez: Adventures of a Physicist* (New York: Basic Books, 1987), 169.
6. Goodchild, *J. Robert Oppenheimer*, 197.
7. *In the Matter of J. Robert Oppenheimer: Transcript of Hearing*, 242–243.
8. Jungk, *Brighter Than a Thousand Suns*, 278.
9. Ibid., 279.
10. Ibid., 280.
11. Alvarez, *Alvarez*, 172.
12. *In the Matter of J. Robert Oppenheimer: Transcript of Hearing*, 77.
13. Philip M. Stern and Harold P. Green, *The Oppenheimer Case: Security on Trial* (New York: Harper & Row, 1969), 143.
14. *In the Matter of J. Robert Oppenheimer: Transcript of Hearing*, 238.
15. Ibid., 79.
16. Ibid.
17. Jungk, *Brighter Than a Thousand Suns*, 285.
18. Goodchild, *J. Robert Oppenheimer*, 204.
19. William J. Broad, "Rewriting the History of the H-Bomb," *Science* 218 (November 1982): 769–772.
20. *In the Matter of J. Robert Oppenheimer: Transcript of Hearing*, 251.

CHAPTER 15

1. *In the Matter of J. Robert Oppenheimer: Transcript of Hearing*, 838.
2. Goodchild, *J. Robert Oppenheimer*, 226.
3. Stern and Green, *The Oppenheimer Case*, 232.
4. *In the Matter of J. Robert Oppenheimer: Transcript of Hearing*, 7.
5. Ibid., 20.

CHAPTER 16

1. *In the Matter of J. Robert Oppenheimer: Transcript of Hearing*, 20.
2. Ibid., 56.
3. Ibid., 118–119.
4. Stern and Green, *The Oppenheimer Case*, 280.

5. *In the Matter of J. Robert Oppenheimer: Transcript of Hearing*, 308.
6. Goodchild, *J. Robert Oppenheimer*, 244.
7. *In the Matter of J. Robert Oppenheimer: Transcript of Hearing*, 165, 167.
8. Ibid., 454.
9. Ibid., 468.
10. Ibid., 565.
11. Goodchild, *J. Robert Oppenheimer*, 251.
12. Alvarez, *Alvarez*, 180.
13. Ibid.
14. *In the Matter of J. Robert Oppenheimer: Transcript of Hearing*, 802–803.
15. Information supplied by Edward Teller.
16. Ibid.
17. *In the Matter of J. Robert Oppenheimer: Transcript of Hearing*, 710.
18. Ibid., 726.

CHAPTER 17

1. U.S. Atomic Energy Commission, *In the Matter of J. Robert Oppenheimer, Text of Principal Documents and Letters*, (U.S. Government Printing Office, Washington, D.C., 1954), 21.
2. Ibid., 13.
3. Goodchild, *J. Robert Oppenheimer*, 261.
4. *In the Matter of J. Robert Oppenheimer: Principal Documents*, 22.
5. Ibid., 23.
6. Ibid.
7. Ibid., 44.
8. Ibid., 45.
9. Ibid.
10. Goodchild, *J. Robert Oppenheimer*, 265.
11. *In the Matter of J. Robert Oppenheimer: Principal Documents*, 51.
12. Ibid., 64.
13. Stern and Green, *The Oppenheimer Case*, 359.
14. John S. Rigden, *Rabi: Scientist and Citizen* (New York: Basic Books, 1987), 230, 231.
15. Stern and Green, *The Oppenheimer Case*, 360.
16. Rigden, *Rabi*, 229.
17. Stern and Green, *The Oppenheimer Case*, 426.

CHAPTER 18

1. Goodchild, *J. Robert Oppenheimer*, 270.
2. Jeremy Bernstein, "Personal History (Physics—Part II)," *The New Yorker* 50 (Feb. 2, 1987): 44.
3. Stern and Green, *The Oppenheimer Case*, 452.

4. Goodchild, *J. Robert Oppenheimer*, 275.
5. Ibid., 276.
6. Ibid., 279.
7. Stern and Green, *The Oppenheimer Case*, 502–503.

CHAPTER 19

1. Gregg Herken, "I. I. Rabi: Mad About the Bomb," *Harper's Magazine* 267 (December 1983): 50–51.
2. Ibid.

Bibliography

BOOKS

Alvarez, Luis W. *Alvarez.* New York: Basic Books, 1987.

Blumberg, Stanley A., and Owens, Gwinn. *Energy and Conflict: The Life and Times of Edward Teller.* New York: G. P. Putnam's Sons, 1976.

Curtis, Charles P. *The Oppenheimer Case: The Trial of a Security System.* New York: Simon and Schuster, 1955.

Fermi, Laura. *Atoms in the Family.* Chicago: University of Chicago Press, 1954.

Goodchild, Peter. *J. Robert Oppenheimer: Shatterer of Worlds.* Boston: Houghton Mifflin, 1980; New York: Fromm International, 1985.

Groueff, Stephane. *Manhattan Project: The Untold Story of the Making of the Atomic Bomb.* New York: Bantam Books, 1967; Boston: Little Brown, 1967.

Groves, Leslie R. *Now It Can Be Told.* New York: Harper & Row, 1962.

Hersey, John. *Hiroshima.* Reprint. New York: Bantam Books, 1959.

Hewlett, Richard G., and Anderson, Oscar E., Jr., *The new world 1939/1946: Vol. 1 of a History of the U.S. Atomic Energy Commission.* University Park, Pa.: Pennsylvania State University Press, 1962.

In the Matter of J. Robert Oppenheimer: Transcript of Hearing Before Personnel Security Board. Washington, D.C., U.S. Government Printing Office, 1954.

In the Matter of J. Robert Oppenheimer: Text of Principal Documents. Washington, D.C.: U.S. Government Printing Office, 1954.

Jungk, Robert, *Brighter Than a Thousand Suns.* New York: Harcourt, Brace and Co., 1956.

Lamont, Lansing. *Day of Trinity.* New York: Atheneum, 1965.

Laurence, William L. *Men and Atoms.* New York: Simon and Schuster, 1959.

Lilienthal, David E. *The Journals of David E. Lilienthal: The Atomic Energy Years, 1945–1950.* New York: Harper & Row, 1964.

Los Alamos 1943–1945: The Beginning of an Era. Los Alamos, N.M.: Los Alamos National Laboratory, 1984.

Michelmore, Peter. *The Swift Years: The Robert Oppenheimer Story.* New York: Dodd Mead & Co., 1969.

Pais, Abraham, Rabi, Isidor I., Seaborg, Glenn T., Serber, Robert, and Weisskopf, Victor F. *Oppenheimer.* New York: Charles Scribner's Sons, 1969.

Rhodes, Richard. *The Making of the Atomic Bomb.* New York: Simon and Schuster, 1986.

Rigden, John S. *Rabi: Scientist and Citizen.* New York: Basic Books, 1987.

Robert Oppenheimer: Letters and Recollections. Edited by Alice Kimball Smith and Charles Weiner. Reprint. Cambridge, Mass.: Harvard University Press, 1980.

Stern, Philip M., with Green, Harold P. *The Oppenheimer Case: Security on Trial.* New York: Harper & Row, 1969.

MAGAZINES

Bernstein, Jeremy. "Personal History (Physics—Part II)." *The New Yorker* 50 (Feb. 2, 1987): 39–69.

Bernstein, Barton J. "The Oppenheimer Conspiracy." *Discover* 6 (March 1985): 22–29.

Broad, William J. "Rewriting the History of the H-Bomb." *Science* 218 (November 1982): 769–772.

Herken, Gregg. "I. I. Rabi: Mad about the Bomb." *Harper's Magazine* 267 (December 1983): 48–55.

INTERVIEWS

Kuhn, Thomas S. Interview with J. Robert Oppenheimer. On file with the Archive for the History of Quantum Physics at the University of California, Berkeley, and the American Institute of Physics, New York.

Index